THE JEWISH AMERICAN
PRINCESS
Handbook

"We're not spoiled, just selective"

WRITTEN BY

DEBBIE LUKATSKY
SANDY BARNETT TOBACK

ILLUSTRATED BY

DEBBIE MACKALL

PRODUCED BY

RAY STROBEL

ISBN: 0-943084-02-4

First printing August 1982

10   9   8   7   6   5   4   3   2   1

Manufactured in the United States of America

Turnbull & Willoughby Books are published by Printed Matter Publishing Co., Inc., 15 N. Arlington Hts. Road, Arlington Hts., Ill. 60004.

Cover photo by:
Robert Ringham

Cover Princess:
Cathy Nissen

Acknowledgements

Our many thanks to the following individuals who were of great assistance in the preparation of this Handbook. Their photographs, ideas, dark secrets from their Prince or Princess years and, of course, their ubiquitous Princess jokes have made this a better book. Our special thanks to William Rodriguez whose inspiration started this whole project and to Sandy Moltz who recommended the two authors to the publisher.

Edith Abramson
Marion Ambrose
Bernice Barnett
Murry Barnett
Ricky Barnett
Michael Beck
Mike Becker
Scott Becker
Renee Becker
Robin Braver
Rhonda Brodes
Monica Bronski
Gayle Brown
Maureen Karon Byron
Gina Catalano
Howard Draft
Adrienne Feigenbaum
    Drucker
Alan Drucker
Joan Esposito
Susan Ficaro
Steve Fossler
Craig Foster
Marsha Garlovsky
Carol Goldstein
Jill Rosenblatt Gordon
Joan Greenfield
Gary Greenspan
Mary Jo Geary
Melissa Geary
Michael Geary
Sandy Happ
Nanci Heller
William Hootnick

Steve Jones
Linda Katz
Rich Klapow
Kobs & Brady
Hilarie Kaufman Kurian
Amy Lapine
Sid Liebenson
Sharon Liss
Amy Liss
Carrie Liss
Marcy Lukatsky
Neeny Lukatsky
Sheryl Lukatsky
Sonny Lukatsky
Cheri Nabat
Cathy Nissen
Sherrie Nissen
Bruce Mason
Michael Mervis
Helene Paradise
Neal Price
Merrill Braver Quintero
Helen Schneider
Barbara Schwartz
Karen Seigel
Beth Sered
Hildy Feinberg Sheinbaum
Marla Simon
Carol Algrhen Snitzer
Stagger Lee's
Lorena Strobel
Alan Tobak
Doug Tumin
Jeff Wellek

Also:
Cheri Abelstein
Nancy Schachtel
Adie Matthews
Betty Schachtel
Beth Schachtel
Melanie Turner
Selma Horn
Elliot Fischoff
Laura Marie
Tess Schlonsky
Harry Kahn
Yvonne Furth
Mr. B
Sari Zimbler
Jody Wilner
Randy Kahan
Craig Katz
Sarah Dempsey
Nancy Nelson
Sandy Kalantzis

CONTENTS

CHAPTER IV

The Great Escape
THE URBAN PRINCESS

From the Lap of Luxury to the Rehab Realm

CHAPTER V

The Designer Dictate
DRESSING FOR SUCCESS

From Clothes to Nose

CHAPTER VI

The Princess' Wedding
THE MAIN EVENT

Good-bye Columbus

CHAPTER VII

Sadie, Sadie,
Married Lady

PRINCESS AS QUEEN

The Promised Land

CHAPTER VIII

You don't have to be
Jewish

DICTIONARY OF JEWISH JARGON

Can a Gentile Relate?

Once upon a time in the faraway kingdom of Suburbia a Princess was born. But she was a mieskeit. Her hair was dark and frizzy. Her eyes were small and squinty.

Because this was a Royal Birth, the good fairies of the land came to bestow presents. First came the good fairy of Bonwit's beauty salon and gave the little princess waist-length, Scandinavian-blonde, poker-straight hair. Next, the good fairy of Mount Sinai Nose Clinic gave the little princess Mitzi Gaynor's nose. Finally, the good fairy of House of Vision fashioned grey-green contact lenses for the little Princess to help her better to see the faraway lands from whence her Prince would come to rescue her . . . but that's another story!

The moral of this story is:

Jewish Princesses are made, not born!

Turn the page for the guide that will unlock for you, all the secrets of this Menonite Mystique . . .

CHAPTER 1

Genesis

BORN WITH A GOLDEN SPOON

The Root of All Guilt

BORN WITH A GOLDEN SPOON

The newborn Princess. From birth she gets used to having her own way. Her doting parents anticipate her every whim. They outfit her in frilly dresses and surround her with a menagerie of cuddly stuffed toys. By the time she is toddling she is no stranger to the children's department at Saks, where one little cry and mother will trade the pink sunsuit for yellow.

Her parents anticipate her every accomplishment . . . her first tooth, first step and her first word. They eagerly await the future when they will have the first dance at her wedding.

Having tackled the task of wrapping her parents around her little finger, she will move on to bigger and better things. The Princess will become a master of manipulation which will serve her well in later years. Already she is beginning to cultivate her charm of knowing when to kvetch and when to cajole.

Q. How do you tickle a Jewish Princess?
A. Gucci, Gucci, goo.

CHOOSING THE ROYAL TITLE

In addition to the name by which she will be known to the general public, the Princess also receives a special Hebrew name at birth. The name is derived from a combination of the names of dearly departed ancestors. But she shouldn't despair if she is named Shelo-mous Shandel after Grandpa Seymour and Great Aunt Sophie. These Hebrew names will ony be used twice . . . at her Bar Mitzvah and her wedding. The rest of the time everyone will know her as Sheryl Sue.

A-DOZEN ADORABLE NAMES		TEN NAMES NEVER CONSIDERED FOR A PRINCESS	
Rhonda	Rachael	Mary	Mary Jane
Sandra	Marla	Jane	Mary Ellen
Fern	Michelle	Ellen	Mary Beth
Amy	Hildi	Beth	Mary Louise
Debbie	Stacey	Louise	
Karen	Myra	And any other combination of the above.	

THE "MISHPOCHA"

Pictures in the Family Gallery

UNCLE LOU

AUNT IDA

Born in a *shtetle,* came to America steerage class at the age of three. Realized the Jewish American dream by becoming President of his own wholesale wine business. Loved and admired not only for supplying the Carmel and Manachevits for the holidays, but also for giving all the nephews summer jobs.

Jilted by a fighter ace in WWII, Aunt Ida married the *boychik* next door instead. While it was no great love match at least he was Jewish. Her Moishe made a fortune in the dry cleaning business and their son Sol succumbed to Aunt Ida's *draying* to become the only Jewish commercial pilot in America.

Mishpocha means family, and family means a 50 person caucus awaiting every move the Princess considers making. Of course each member of the mishpocha has a different opinion. The only thing they can agree upon is that they will never agree. All of these decision makers, grandparents, aunts, uncles and cousins each has a colorful past which helps shape the Princess' personality. But the Princess listens to their advice only when she wants, for like each of them, she has a mind of her own.

Below are four photos from the Princess' family album. Take a closer look and you'll probably note the resemblence to someone in your family. An Uncle Lou by any other name is still a gonsa kanocker*.

AUNT MOLLY   *COUSIN IRA*

Broke with tradition by arranging her own marriage in the old country which started her illustrious career as a matchmaker. Never mind that most of her "catches" are balding and still live at home. When you see her coming you flee in panic while she admonishes, "but he's good to his mother".

Graduated magna cum laude Harvard '68; Harvard Law, '71. Married a *shiksa,* Mary O'Brien, at St. Patrick's June '72. Sired son Sean September '72. Aunt Molly still won't believe the scandal. She's still passing out Ira's phone number at the beauty shop "just in case".

*Gonsa Kanocker: Big shot.

THE FINELY FURNISHED FRONTROOM

1) Picture window with swagged brocade drapes and valances
2) Walls papered in white silk moire
3) Japanese silkscreen scrolls
4) Limoges vases
5) Lladro figurines
6) Lalique crystal ashtrays
7) Rose velour Louis XIV sofa (slipcovered in plastic)
8) One dozen gold fringed, cut velvet pillows
9) Cut velvet wing chairs in same fabric as pillows
10) Smoked glass credenza containing crystal serving pieces in Waterford's Lismore, silver service for twelve of Wallace's Grand Baroque and Wedgewood's Jasper
11) White brick woodburning fireplace housing dried silk flower arrangement
12) Oriental TV console with non-working television inside
13) Silver loving cup won by Grandma Minnie in 1923 at

During the Palace Years, when the Princess was growing up, this was the one room in the house that no one ever entered. Even the Princess, who was denied nothing, was not allowed to set foot inside. With its museum-quality furniture and assorted chazeri, this room was so off-limits that the Princess could even imagine a velvet rope separating it from curious onlookers.

Far Rockaway Independence Day Beauty Pagent, filled with a dried silk flower arrangement

14) Marble topped coffee table with claw legs

15) Crystal candy dish filled with Barton's hard candy

16) More Lladro

17) Leather-bound album — "Our Wedding"

19) Three tiered crystal chandelier

20) Oriental end tables

21) More Lladro

22) Handpainted china lamp with organdy shade covered in plastic

23) Matching handpainted lamp. You thought one would be enough?

24) Impressionist oil painting (authentic imitation)

25) More of the same, matted in cut velvet

26) Wall sconces patterned in gold leaf

HADASSAH BAROQUE

The Heritage of Overdecorating

As the Princess was growing up her mother's home was so overdecorated it was the envy of the entire *Hadassah* group. Mother's motto was:

This motto applied to every-thing from flocked chairs to china poodles, from gilt frames to wall sconces. The preferred shades in the most fashionable homes were gold and avocado green. Perhaps these colors weren't very stunning but who's to argue with suburbs full of Jewish housewives?

Plastic slipcovers were de rigeur as were tracks from the vacuum cleaner which dictated the traffic pattern throughout the house.

VARIATIONS ON VELOUR

THE PLASTIQUE MYSTIQUE

Early in her life the Princess learned that the favored fabric for furniture was velour because of its many fine qualities. It's showy, comes in many colors, shows off crystal to its best advantage and nicely compliments the flocked wallpaper and gilt frames. In fact, the virtues of velour are so numerous that the Princess' mother was willing to overlook the fact that, not only did the sofa pillows need constant fluffing and plumping, but they attracted dust like a magnet.

Stemming from the days when bubbie wrapped all the leftovers in waxed paper, the Jewish mother tried to keep her palace looking fresh as well by wrapping all the fine furniture in plastic. Everything was slipcovered, from kitchen to dining room, and only unveiled when company came. Just what constituted company was never determined, however. To date, no one has rated a seat on bare velour. Maybe when the Princess brings home a prospective Prince.

"Just last week my mother realized that, not only could you see the cushions on the sofa, but there was actually room to sit down! Seeing a chance to turn a problem into an opportunity, Mom immediately went to her favorite department store where she spotted some pillows which were perfect for filling the void. But they only had FOUR, can you imagine? I tell you she needed at least a dozen. To buy, or not to buy ... that was the question.

It's no wonder from all this that I go for track lights and Levelors. I'm into high tech, not high drech."

Mrs. A. Blum
Shaker Heights

GOLDFISH GOLDFARB AND OTHER MAINTENANCE-FREE PETS

Although the young Princess craves four-legged companionship, a big dog is just not her style (besides, her mother would never let it in the house). For this reason the favored breed is the miniature poodle, with hair that can be coiffed and nails manicured. The yorkie runs a close second as the preferred pet, with hair that takes so nicely to barrettes and bows that shedding can be overlooked.

Because the Princess has a weakness for things 24K, goldfish are also favored pets. With minimal upkeep and no fur to shed they are a welcome addition to any Princess' palace.

The pets with the most show and the least go are stuffed animals. Here size doesn't matter. From a tiny teddy to a giant giraffe from FAO Schwartz, each has a name and a personality. And, they have a lifespan that lasts as long as mother's patience for dusting them does.

GLOSSARY OF PET NAMES

Poochie   This name is also popular for hot dog stands

Goochie   Louis Vuitton has too many syllables

Bagel   You wouldn't want to say, "Here cream cheese". Lox is too expensive.

Velvet   Not gold or avocado green, but lovely for poodles, none the less.

Martini   A Princess certainly wouldn't drink one!

Jezebel   Even the best homes have one.

Muffy   For the Prep pup.

HEBREW SCHOOL

After nine years of giving in to their Princess' evey whim her parents finally work up enough courage to make her do something she really doesn't want to do. With promises of great Bat Mitzvah gifts the Princess is coerced into spending three afternoons a week at the neighborhood Hebrew school. Here she will learn all about the customs and traditions of her people while learning how to read just enough Hebrew to get through her Haftorah and the high holidays. If the Princess would spend as much time learning to write Hebrew as she did writing notes to her friend Helene, she'd really grow up to be a big macher in the temple.

Perfect Princesses

The early years are coming to a close as our little Princess has been thoroughly spoiled by her parents. The groundwork has been laid and she is ready to follow in her older sister's footsteps and become a Princess-in-Training.

As she marches into the Minor Leagues her miniature Louis Vuitton bag has already taken on the appearance it will have in later life: full of play money and daddy's expired credit cards.

Although she can't understand her older sister's newfound interest in the opposite sex she admires her superior manipulative powers and already realizes she has a long way to go on the road to fulfilling her heritage of becoming a true Princess.

Once upon a time there lived a Princess named Hindarella and her two squabbling siblings, brother Barry and sister Sari. Barry was a mischievious 12 year old with a penchant for pestering Hindarella everytime she got to the phone. Sari was a sophisticated 28, who retired from teaching to marry a dentist and cultivate carats.

One typical Friday night, as the family was gathered around the **Shabbos** table, Hindarella announced they were also having her new beau, Scott Silver, for dinner. The family took her a little too literally and Scott was chewed up, but good!

Barry started in on him immediately by asking if Scott liked baseball 'cause he'd heard Scott had gotten to 3rd base. Sari didn't waste a minute in complementing Hindarella, "That sweater looks almost as good on you as it did on me last year. Red is really your shade." Mother and Father got their portion, too. "So Scott, what does your father do?" As Barry chimed in, "Is he an acrobat in the circus? I heard Hinda say he's rolling in it." Then Sari took one last

bite and whined, "Mother, this tenderloin is delicious, but how come we only had brisket when I first brought Arnold home?"

Hindarella, ever the clever princess, knew she had to save Scott from being boiled alive in his **tepel.** Jumping up from the table, exclaiming that if they left **immediately** they'd just make the 8:00 show. She muttered under her breath to Barry on her way out, "Sorry sucker, since you're all wet, you get stuck with the dishes!"

The moral of this story?
Although blood, not water, may be thicker, you can never win when fighting with your sister!

CHAPTER 2

The Minor Leagues

PRINCESS-IN-TRAINING

Acceptance by the Tribe

PRINCESS-IN-TRAINING
The Early Years

As the Princess enters her teens the pre-nuptial practice begins with her Bat Mitzvah and continues with her Sweet 16. During this period she learns behavior becoming to a Princess like smiling graciously when opening gifts she really can't stand and planning democratic seating arrangements.

Her parents begin to feel their grip on their little Princess loosening especially when she plucks her first Forbidden Fruit.

TRIBAL RITES
A Time to See and Be Seen

TISHREI					5738	
			1	2	3	4
5	6	7	8	9	10	11
12	13	14	15	16	17	18
19	20	21	22	23	24	25
26	27	28	29	30	31	

Of course, one of the major aspects of the young Princess' upbringing is learning to carry on Jewish traditions. But for the Princess, the many religious holidays are not only a time rich in celebration and tradition but also an opportunity to see and be seen.

Of course, one of the major aspects of the young Princess' upbringing is learning to carry on Jewish traditions. But for the Princess, the many religious holidays are not only a time rich in celebration and tradition but also an opportunity to see and be seen.

SHABAT SHALOM

As everyone knows, God created the universe in six days and on the seventh day he rested. As you can imagine, the Princess needs a weekly rest too, from the stresses of shopping and tennis. The Sabbath is welcomed with chicken soup and brisket. But the tradition of the Sabbath guest is most important . . . particularly if he is the eligible son of a wealthy neighbor.

ROSH HASHANA

This is a holiday which has a four-fold meaning:

1. It is the New Year . . . you wouldn't be caught *dead* showing up at temple in last year's Halston.

2. It is the day of remembrance . . . remembering if anyone is wearing last year's Loehmann's.

3. It is the day of Judgement . . . time to judge if anyone is looking chicer than you.

4. Finally, it is the day for blowing the Shofar
After all, this is what temple is for, isn't it?

HANUKAH

Dear Chanukah Fairy,

I've really been the perfect little princess this year. I've written to my grandma in Miami Beach every week, and I haven't overslept Sunday School once. Here are a few things I'd like for Chanukah. A little fur jacket, a Gucci belt, a Louis Vuitton bag, a pair of Andrew Geller boots, a Rolex watch, a trip to Acapulco, a pair of diamond stud earrings and a rich doctor for when I grow up.

Thank you very much.
Love, Rhonda

YOM KIPPUR

On this day, the day of Attonement, the Princess, who is always quick to judge others, must herself be judged. On the plus side, she has been good to her mother and grateful to her father; but she did treat Alan Drucker shamelessly, and then there's Lynn's blouse she thought about never returning . . . and how about that Meyer's bag her mother thinks she got wholesale? Just wait 'till dad sees the bill!

PASSOVER

This is the holiday that meant freedom for the Princess' ancestors. Passover is a holiday rich in symbolism as depicted on the Seder Plate shown below. And don't forget to leave the door open for Elijah, you never know, he might have a cute friend for you!

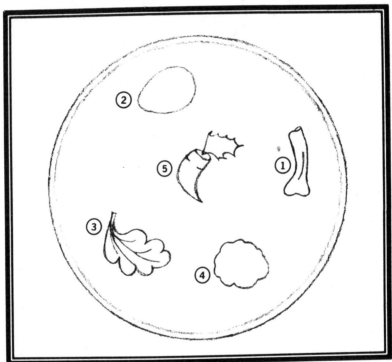

①Roasted shank bone of lamb.
Origin of the curly lamb coat.

②Hard boiled egg
Reminiscent in shape of the oval cut diamond. Usually matching in size the one the Princess hopes, one day, to have on her hand.

③Bitter Herbs
Great for the sinuses but they won't do anything for a deviated septum.

④Charoses
Equals one Weight Watcher's fruit exchange

⑤Karpas
Parsley, celery or lettuce may be used. Fill up on these caloric bargains.

The Bat Mitzvah
THE CROWNING EVENT

The *Bat Mitzvah* marks the Princess' emergence into womanhood and it is also good practice for that day in the future when she will once again stand in front of the Rabbi. Because the Princess has spent months learning her *Haftorah* and her mother making preparations, this day is choreographed down to the last detail.

8:00 AM — Wake up — too nervous to sleep

9:00 AM — Fight with your mother

9:30 AM — Beauty shop appointment

10:00 AM — Fight with hairdresser. Mother told him to pull your hair off your face, you want bangs

10:00 AM — Compromise — one side pulled back

10:30 AM — Manicure

10:35 AM — Fight with mother — you choose Cadillac Red, she says Misty Mauve

10:45 AM — *Compromise: Wine with Everything.*

11:00 AM — Try on lipsticks, and wait for mother to finish up

12:00 Nn — Too nervous for lunch (this should happen every day)

1:00 PM — Fight with mother. It's been an hour since the last one

5:00 PM — Where did the time go, you'll never make it to the temple by 7:00

5:30 PM — Run pantyhose while dressing, PANIC. Send father to drugstore for new pair

6:00 PM — He's back with the only color they had: Suntan Taupe.

6:05 PM — You cry and fight with mother. She says they're fine, no one will notice!

6:06 PM — You cry harder . . . you must have Seashell.

6:07 PM — She gives you her hose. "I sacrifice my life for you!" Creme Crepe . . . they'll do.

6:15 PM — HAIR we go again! Too Painful to elaborate.

6:30 PM — Leave for temple.

6:36 PM — Turn back — left haftorah at home.

7:05 PM — Arrive at temple late — Jewish Standard Time. Not even time to fight with your mother.

7:07 PM — Service — believe it or not, all goes well.

8:59 PM — Service ends — fight with your mother.

9:00 PM — Receiving line — pre-nuptual practice.

9:15 PM — Oneg Shabat.

11:00 PM — In bed too nervous to sleep, already worrying about tomorrow night's party.

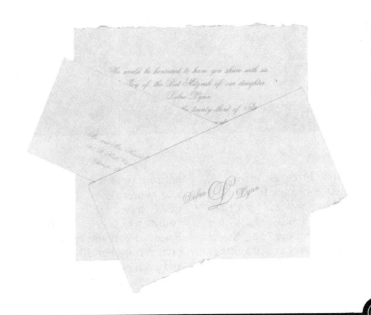

"SWEET SIXTEEN AND NEVER BEEN KISSED"

Does Mother have to know all the details?

As the Princess turns 16, mother gets a chance to throw a gala party to show off to all her friends what a little lady her Princess has become. The Sweet 16 party also serves as still another dress rehearsal for the Princess' Wedding Day.

After choosing an impossibly cute theme, the princess spends an entire day looking for invitations and centerpieces. The florist suggests mock sodas made from mums which coordinate with the Sweet 16 theme. The Princess invites only her 50 *closest* friends and even includes her creepy cousin Rhoda. The guest list is usually good for at least a couple of battles with mother.

After the invitations are out, the Princess starts to case Bonwit's and Saks for an outfit befitting the occasion. Mother and daughter compromise somewhere between precious/cute and trendy/sophisticate.

All this planning culminates in a lovely luncheon where the Princess receives loads of presents. (Why else invite 50 people?) These gifts usually run the gamut from cute tops and nightgowns to the requisite gold bangle bracelet and ring with a fair-sized stone. It becomes obvious as the Princess displays all the loot that this is merely a training ground for that magical day in the future when Prince Charming sweeps her off her feet and under the *chuppa*.

But the ultimate gift, too big to wrap, comes from mom and dad. The gift is, of course, a set of keys to her very own sporty Camaro or Firebird, in the favored colors of red or yellow. These keys to the kingdom will give her parents many sleepless nights but no self respecting Princess would be caught *dead* riding the bus to school once she's turned 16.

FORBIDDEN FRUITS or

INTERFAITH DATING

Having learned nothing from the lesson of the Garden of Eden, the Princess is known to indulge in a forbidden fruit or two of her own.

The Princess' life is carefully planned so that she knows she must someday marry a "NJB" (nice Jewish boy). For this reason she finds it enticing to date a Gentile boy . . . one her parents would never approve of. The lure of blond hair, blue eyes and a one syllable last name are just too powerful to resist. Basketball games at other high schools provide the most fertile hunting ground for these desirable catches and, once the bait is set, it's too late to turn back.

These Gentile boys find the Princesses an exotic breed, one which likes to have the car door opened for them and one which would rather dehydrate before drinking a beer. These Pats and Chucks love having the chance to drive around in her Firebird or Camaro and, best of all, they never have to meet her parents.

Once her parents **do** find out, the Princess' forbidden fruit becomes even more alluring. Everything the Princess does that displeases her parents is blamed on Tim (Pat, John, etc.). They notice she's eating creamed chipped beef on toast, wearing lots of Tartan plaid and sending for brochures from DeVry Tech.

Yelling and pleading, making threats and even giving guilt do nothing to persuade the Princess to give up her knight (albeit a tarnished one). Only when her parents finally decide to relent and accept what they're hoping is temporary insanity does the Princess forsake her Forbidden Fruit and seek someone who thinks more like she does . . . college and Med school.

> **Dinner-and-a-Show Syndrome:** Affliction common to those who date Princesses. A form of foreplay whereby one must wine and dine the Princess before being allowed to lay even one hand on her precious lily-white body. (It will probably be rebuffed anyway.) Symptoms include eating a dinner-and-a-half (Princesses only pick), consuming quantities of mega-calorie desserts and suffering through a torrent of Neil Simon movies. The only known cure for this malady is to start dating *shiksas*.

THE CURFEW CRISIS
Mother Knows Best

Now that she is mobile the Princess indulges in later hours ... but just what are later hours? Mom and dad lay down the law with a manditory curfew. No matter what time is set for the curfew the Princess feels it is too early and she'll be leaving just when all the fun begins. She finds a way around this, however, by bringing Freddy home for some heavy duty making out in the den. A few nights of this and her parents finally agree to a later curfew. Freddy doesn't understand why she's dropped him so quickly but figures it's just part of the Princess charm.

"I give my parents more credit than the rest. While my girlfriends Cindy and Toby moaned about their early curfews, I couldn't resist bragging about my lack of one. My parents never said more than, "Not too late'. I can't tell you how long it took me to catch on. When everyone else had to be home by 10:00, what's a poor Princess to do but go home too!"

Marcy P.
Roslyn, Long Island

WHEN I REMEMBERED MAMA

There are those who say God couldn't be everywhere, so he created the Jewish mother. And, of course, it's true she's omnipotent too. Just when the fun's about to begin the Princess envisions her mother's admonishing look.

Places God Couldn't Be

If the young Princess-in-Training ever finds herself in any of these compromising situations she needn't worry ... she's only hearing the voice of her conscience, not her mother.

1. She's in the throes of a passionate embrace that's threatening to "come between her and her Calvin's".

2. She's planning on a Miami vacation. Why does it have to be spent at grandma Birdie's condo?

3. Her fork is poised over an enormous piece of Junior's cheesecake, with hot fudge yet.

4. She's signing $75.00 over to Elizabeth Arden for "Bette Davis Eyes".

5. She's at Sassoon about to go from Mousey Menonite to Sunny Shiske.

GELT
WITHOUT GUILT

**As the Princess grows up she learns that not everything in life is free
and, for this reason, God created credit cards.**

At birth a Princess is given many generous gifts of savings bonds and checks. Unfortunately, she cannot touch any of this gelt which is so essential to her acquiring of gilt. So she must find another source of income. Grandma and grandpa are good for only so much, like Hershey bars and hair ribbons, and their gifts of gelt can't keep up with the Princess' increasingly expensive tastes.

Her first lesson in enlarging her buying power comes from her mother who never pays with cash, but with plastic.

The Princess must use all her ingenuity to keep her father from having heart failure when the bills arrive. Following are just a few of her most effective ploys:

THE STING
Have the saleslady remove all the tags so daddy doesn't see the damage until it's too late.
THE SHELL GAME
Buy your Polos in the little boy's department. When your father sees them tell him they're your little brother's.

THE FLEECE

Spread out your spending. When running up a $500.00 bill at Magnin's take home only half and have the rest delivered on a weekday when daddy's at work.

3 CARD MONTE

Don't charge all of your purchases at one place. Bonwit's, Bloomingdales and Bendel's all carry Anne Klein.

BAIT & SWITCH

Buy a little something for dad. While he's admiring his gift, sneak your packages up to your room.

Lest you think the Princess mercenary it must be understood that she engages in this spending selflessly.

She knows nothing makes daddy happier than to see his Princess enjoying all the privileges he never had and only he can give her. Also, it gives him something to boast about when all the other fathers are *joyously complaining* about how much their daughters are spending. And *nothing* makes daddy dig down deeper than if the Princess actually goes out and gets a part time job (an acceptable one, of course) and earns a little pin money of her own.

ACCEPTABLE JOBS	UNACCEPTABLE JOBS
Salesgirl at Bergdorf's Runner at Commodities Exchange JCC daycamp counselor	Waitress Counter girl at any fast food chain Checker at grocery store

Many years have passed and now it is time for the Princess to leave for college. The good fairies who have graced the Princess with a quick mind and an astronomical SAT score have also bestowed upon her a well written application essay highlighting her accomplishments to date. The good fairy of student politics has seen to it that the Princess has held every elective office from hall monitor to Student Council President. But, just in case, her father has a "connection" on every Admissions Board in the country.

Perusing the catalogs and brochures, the Princess envisions the far away campus from whence her Prince will come. But that's another story . . .

Onward then, the Princess goes to college.

CHAPTER 3

Exodus

OFF TO COLLEGE

The Long Road to Mecca

SCOUTING FOR SCHOOLS
The Legend of the Alma Mater

*This poor woman has been standing for centuries
and chances are, she'll never get a rest.
According to legend the Alma Mater will only sit down
when a Princess graduates a virgin.*

By this time every Princess knows she is meant for the best life has to offer so she must be very careful about choosing the best college at which to spend the next four years (Princesses *always* graduate on time). The two most important considerations in selecting a school are the caliber of the education she will receive and the caliber of the potential mates she will find there. Then, there are the secondary concerns: proximity to shopping, sororities and social life.

Herewith are the Top Ten schools for husband hunters. All vital statistics are included to help you choose the school (and Prince) that's right for you.

American University:
Washington, D.C. (2,652 men, 2,498 women) Good for meeting politicians. Washington hostess is an admirable profession. Pack your "I voted for Anderson" button, an evening dress and your Gucci clutch. Bone up on cocktail party chatter before you go.

Arizona State:
Tempe, AZ. Also known as Suntan U. (10,899 men, 8,622 women) 5 year plan. Noted for its arrid climate. Preferred major is pre-father's business. Pack your reflector and good moisturizer. 12,000 Trans Ams on campus, all with out-of-state plates.

University of Miami:
Coral Gables, FL. (4,916 men, 3,360 women) Great clime. Noted for its proximity to the Bal Harbour shops. Campus reeks of Bain de Soleil. Pack a scarf and sunglasses for convertible capers. Only competition here is for lawn chairs. Breeding ground for bronzed post-grads.

NYU:
The Big Apple (3,500 men, 3,500 women) Bloomie's, Bendel's and Bergdorf's . . . need we say more? Pack your charge cards. The competition here is really stiff, with only one Prince for every Princess.

Northwestern University:
Evanston, IL. (3,832 men, 2,928 women) Noted for academic excellence. Look for love over chili-burgers at J.K. Sweets. First choice for fur clad Princesses as Winters can last 10 months. Great for indoor sports. Pack your books . . . people actually *study* here.

Ohio State:
Columbus, OH. (22,012 men, 17,188 women) Heavy on Greek. Best ZBTs anywhere. Sammies not bad either. Go Deephers. Never make it to class if you cross the Oval. Pack your Vuitton weekender and matching garment bag.

Syracuse:
Syracuse, N.Y. (6,032 men, 4,808 women) 90% of student body had nose jobs. Classes cancelled for high holidays.

Sophie Newcomb:
New Orleans, LA. (All girls but S.N. shares the Tulane campus.) Tulane and Jew Lane, all in one town. With 3,104 men it's a non-stop social life. Formals every weekend. Big league JAPS, all in AEPhi and SDT. Dates with big spenders and all that Jazz. Students leave town for Mardi Gras.

U.C.L.A.:
Berkley, CA. (12,125 men, 8,671 women) Great place for learning about investments. Start immediately investing in your future by being seen in Beverly Hills. Pack your funkiest fashions and a fur for

February when the mercury hits 50. Upon arrival on campus, open an account at Georgio's.

Washington University:
St. Louis, MO. (2,500 men, 1,850 women) For serious students so you know he'll make a good living. Don't pack anything...there's nothing to do in St. Louis.

FORBIDDEN FRUITS

Southern Methodist University:
No N.J.B.s here . . .

Brigham Young University:
None here either.

Lake Forest College:
You want a Prince, not a Prep.

Bennington:
Too artsy-fartsy. You'll never meet a decent Prince here.

M.I.T.:
Not unless you're into slide rules.

Mount Holyoke:
All women and none of them Princesses.

University of Utah:
Can't risk messing up a surgeon's handiwork on the slopes.

University of Vermont:
Can only shop from catalogs here . . . too hard for returning.

DeVry Tech:
The technological age may be the third wave but it would be too much of a shock to the Princess' future.

"A" w/o EFFORT

Keep up your social life while keeping up your grades as well. By taking these courses you're not only guaranteed an "A" but you get a chance to meet all the N.J.B.s on campus as well.

1. Cultivating Carats (Geology for JAPS)

2. JAPanese Tea Ceremony (Oriental Art)

3. Cannibis Rex (Literature for Druggies)

4. The Goyish Gavotte (Ballroom Dancing)

5. From Bexley to Broadway (Introduction to Theater)

TESTIMONIAL
FROM A NEW ARRIVAL

As I arrived on campus I realized that my early Princess training would serve me well for I was now used to having my own way. After an 8 hour drive in a car packed so full that I had to squeeze up front with mommy and daddy, we finally arrived at the dorm to which I had been assigned. In a six story dorm with an elevator that only went up to five, I was assigned to room #610. My father found a cute Senior boy to help him schlepp my countless trunks and paraphernalia. I was a great help, standing on the sidelines trying to get the Senior to ask for my phone number.

I was anxious to meet my roommate (with whom I could share closet space and boyfriends) but I didn't wait around for a formal introduction. For there she was, caught in Kodacolor, framed for posterity in front of a Christmas tree with her grandmother who could have been straight out of American Gothic. *Where* was Myra Stein? If this wasn't enough, our tiny room had only one small closet! A nightmare for me and my

S'Fantastic shoes, Young New Yorker nightwear and Miss Magnin culottes

So, we schlepped back down, lock, stock and baggage. My father reloaded the car and I whined all the way to University Housing.

Their suggestion — a metal closet in the hall — made me cry even louder. "They'll steal all of my clothes! I'm *not* getting dressed in the hall!" Attempting to calm me down they offered a University lock for $10 extra to protect all of my treasures. "NO WAY!", I cried.

Then my father stepped in. Lord knows, he couldn't leave his Princess in the hands of these *brutes!* And finally, a new room was found. In a new dorm. A room of my own . . . with *plenty* of closet space.

Fortunately I had arrived on campus early. I could picture the scene at University Housing later in the day when dozens of Princesses and their fathers would be lined up all trying to get *their* way.

Sandy Goldberg
Berkley, CA.

THE
DORM ROOM

1) 9x6 shag carpet remnant to cover indoor-outdoor stuff the room came with.

2) Twin beds with matching spreads, dust ruffles & pillow shams.

3) Twin study pillows

4) Twin digital clock radios

5) Twin tensor study lamps

6) Not enough closet space

7) Built-in desks with coordinated desk set:
   Monogrammed lucite waste basket
   monogrammed lucite blotter
   monogrammed lucite pencil cup
   monogrammed lucite mail caddy

8) Very expensive stereo (reflects

the listener's interest in money)

9) Record album collection: Barry Manilow, Bruce Springsteen, Neil Diamond, Barbara Streisand, The Go-Go's (and anything else that's current), Itzak Perelman and Zuben Mehta at the Met

10) Sign in board from Sweet 16

11) Towel stolen from the Diplomat, Miami Beach

12) Bong with dried silk flower arrangement

13) Make-up mirror, curling iron, electric rollers, blow dryer-and-a-spare

14) Sperti Sunlamp

15) Afghan knitted by Grandma

16) Cases of Tab

17) Address book categorized by Sammies, ZBT and AEPi

18) Marimekko wallhangings

19) Rosmond prints

20) Color TV

21) Princess phone with call waiting and call forwarding

22) Bulletin board with sorority bids, invitations to dances, photos of old high school friends and Springsteen poster

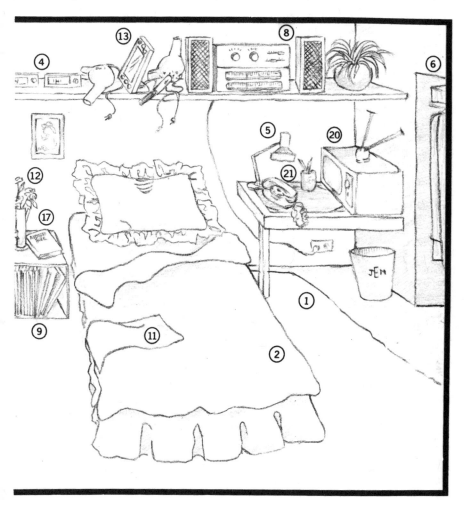

CHOOSING A MAJOR — HIS NOT YOURS

Gone are the days when teaching was the only choice for a nice Jewish girl. Thanks to the women's movement, the Princess now enjoys a much greater variety of options than ever before. Premed, prelaw, and business offer much more potential. She can be a doctor, or date one, she can practice law or court a lawyer. And an MBA is almost as desireable as an MRS.

After the Princess has selected a major, the next major step is selecting her course load. Registration is the first big social event of the season on most campuses. Particularly after winter break when the Princess sports a Miami Beach suntan. It's OK to sign up for courses like Business Administration and Advanced Chemistry because these are the courses that all the Sheldon Rights are taking. If you choose these courses keep in mind that you'll be in for some heavy-duty studying. But don't fret. The library's a great place to meet your match. And what better way to strike up a conversation with someone you could die for, than by asking to borrow his accy notes.

It is very important for the Princess to develop good study habits so she can maintain her stellar gradepoint. Proper tools include one highlighter and a spare, legal pads, pencils and 24 packs of Trident sugarless gum

(NOTE: Phyllis Weiss, Brandeis '73, has been credited with mastering the art of reading assignments with one eye on her books and one scouting for Sammies *and* she managed to go from graduating with honors to honeymoneying with Harvey inside of a semester.)

When scheduling classes, the Princess must make sure she allows herself enough time beforehand to wash and dry her hair, touch up her manicure, do her eyebrows and finish up with electric rollers. She never knows who she might run into on her way to class.

The Princess hates to miss a class. She *is* in college for an education, after all. And, even more important, she might miss an opportunity to meet a Prince. But there are times when the weather's so humid, it just doesn't pay. In this instance, it's perfectly acceptable to call Jordy or Josh or whomever and ask him to bring over his notes later.

The Princess' hard work at school is rewarded with a degree and her entree into the world of business or wedded bliss.

Tear out this handy chart and use for reference.

YOUR MAJOR	PROFESSION	HIS EARNING POWER
Sociology/ Psychology	Social Worker	$15,000 - 29,999*
Business/ Accounting	Accountant/CPA	$22,000 - 59,999**
English/History/ Political Science	Lawyer	$25,000 - 199,999+**
Chemistry, Biology	Doctor	$30,000 - 299,999+**
Finance/Ag Economics	Commodities Broker	Sky's the limit***

* Poor risk — unless he also dabbles in the stock market
**Once in private practice, unlimited earning power
***For those willing to take risks and live on Valium

FORBIDDEN FRUITS

ROTC	Officer in Armed Forces	$ 8,000 - 19,999*
Physical Education/ Health	Gym Teacher	$10,000 - 29,000*
Mathematics	Computer Analyst	$20,000 - 49,999*
Marine Biology	Marine Biologist	$30,000 - 59,999+*
Forensic Studies	Policeman	$20,000 - 69,999*
Aviation	Pilot	$40,000 - 99,999*

*Doesn't matter how much they make. What would a nice Jewish girl want with guys like these?

THE GOLD RUSH

Pledging the Perfect Sorority

Welcome to campus. After a few days the Princess already hates feeling like one of the crowd. The alternative is, of course, going Greek. To some, the Greek system may look like just another crowd but not to the Princess. She's longing to wear the Greek letters on her chest, another badge to show she is one of the chosen.

There are often 20 odd sororities the Princess will see during the rush but it is important for her to remember that only three are worth considering: Alpha Epsilon Phi, Delta Phi Epsilon and Sigma Delta Tau. All of the other sororities are composed of a diversity of girls working and living together. Not so for the Princess' choice. Her sorority will be a homogeneous group . . . a house full of Princess clones, all with identically expensive tastes in everything from fashion to passion.

Rush is a hectic time filled with a lot of fun, a lot of decisions and a lot of phone calls to mother. The Princess will be meeting literally hundreds of new friends (that she'll never talk to again) through her Rush counselors (all blond shicksas from Thetas) and in the sororities she visits. The key to having a good time is for the Princess to be herself. Relax and give every sorority the opportunity to know her. In 95% of the houses she visits this means to ignore the girls after they ask what her father does and the origins of her ancestors.

The Princess then must concentrate on the M&Ms . . . they're non-denominational. Once the Princess has eliminated all of the drecky houses she can get down to the real business at hand.

The most sought after Princesses will be wooed by AEPhi, SDT and Deephers and all have their advantages. Each is a place where Princesses share in each others lives and work together for the betterment of both the group and the individual. Sharing in each others lives means sharing everything from Everclear to Enovid and, when one Princess meets a Zeeb, the whole group benefits. This is an atmosphere which lets each girl make special friends (i.e. clique), develop her talents (rolling the perfect joint) and broaden her college experience (losing her virginity for the first time) and her beam on late night pizzas.

Essay on AEPi

As the old saying goes, "Why buy the bull...?" By senior year the Princess has sown her wild oats and is tired of all the "schmucks" from Sammies and ZBT and is ready for some real "brisket."

As the stars in her eyes turn to dollar signs, she looks to the Alpha Epsilon Pis (AEPi). Their stability, dependability and thoughtfulness that the Princess despised when she was younger and looking for a good time, now seem like admirable traits for a potential prince. AEPi guys are more than ready, willing and able. After all, they've spent the past 3 years' worth of Saturday nights with Penthouse pinups. All the money the've saved on good drugs, fast women and fast cars now pours into the Princess' coffers. They're also willing to part with their fraternity pins. And the Princess proudly wears this badge on her chest until the time **she** is ready to exchange it for a diamond on her finger. While this may not be a match made in heaven, why throw out dirty water until you have clean.

TALE FROM A TOKEN

By the time I got to college, I was really fed up with being just another Princess. I went through rush and knew I could really outshine the shikses. And besides, I always wanted to date a Sigma Chi. So, when I got a bid from the Kappas, I accepted. But believe, me, just like milchik and fleishich, we didn't mix. I alone had to rise at the crack of dawn to blow dry my curls, my turned up nose was not from nature, and baked ham on Sundays was no substitute for bagels and lox. I regained my senses junior year when I got engaged to a Zeeb. The sound of 60 NJB's serenading me with "Sunrise/Sunset" was too much for the Kappas.

Judy Solomon-Stein
Ohio State '76

April at most colleges is time for the Sammies to throw a party for which they're famous (?): a huge dance with a nautical theme, The Sammies Shipwreck Party.

The Chapter House (which already looks like a maritime disaster) is decorated with too much fish netting, too many bouys and seafaring decks (short for decoration). A local band plays the latest New Wave rock and everyone gets drunk on everclear punch. It's a *must* for Freshman Princesses to be asked so they can buy cute navy blue and white sailor outfits. Their Sammie dates all wear Top Siders and the T-shirt favors.

It doesn't matter that the Princess like her date. The idea is to see and be seen. The following day's proper etiquette calls for the Princess not to appear at breakfast thereby keeping everyone guessing. Then it's time to start scouting for the upcoming ZBT dance!

AN INSIDE LOOK*
AT SAMMIES & ZBTs

	SAMMIES	ZBTs
Physical characteristics	Nose jobs, curly hair big biceps, cute little tushies. Roman hands, contacts.	Big tushies, cute little biceps, Mediterranean noses & complexion. Russian fingers, glasses.
Clothes	T-shirts & Levis, Nike running shoes	Plaid pants, saddle shoes, Polo T's
Lovemaking Techniques	Reefer & bunk beds, Frank Zappa & strob lights	Wine & loft beds, Stan Getz & candlelight
Cars	Toyota Celicas Honda Preludes MG	Firebird & Trans Ams, Mazda Rx-7,
Majors	Pre Med Pre Law Accounting	Pre Med Pre Law Accounting

	SAM	ZBT
Best dancers	6.7	4.2
Biggest jerks	8.4	4.3
Best lovers	7.9	5.0
Most intelligent	8.3	8.4
Best manners	6.4	3.9
Most ambition	8.0	7.5
Best personality	6.6	6.9
Greatest drinking capacity	9.2	8.9
Biggest preverts	6.9	9.1

Based on a survey of over 1,800 Princesses and Queens. Mailing list compiled from the Active and Alumni chapters of AEPhi and SDT. Open ended questions were asked (i.e. Describe a typical all-nighter with a Sammie. A ZBT) and all respondents were asked to grade both fraternities, on a scale from 1 to 10, in various categories. The averages were computed and the results are given in the above charts. (Note: Questionnaires were also mailed to 600 Kappas and Thetas. No response has been received thus far.)

Dear Lou,

I just got your letter and I love your Lou stationary. Suzy is going to Champaign to see David so, if I don't have a lot of tests and homework, maybe I'll come down. But when are you going to come here? Sounds like you're having too wild of a time to leave. I finally made it to my first frat party — Sammies Shipwreck. It was wild! I really had a good time. And that was before I took a lude. You know I've always wanted to do the deed with a sailor (just kidding). There were so many cute NJBs there and they were all coming over to meet me. My date was furious but with all those hunks I don't think I'll have to worry for the rest of the year.

I met a millionaire at a bar last weekend. He told me his dad was a diamond broker — hint, hint. Then he asked me to the ZBT pledge dance next week. I'm a little nervous though 'cause I heard they do these skits where they rip everyone up and I'm afraid I'll come out in little pieces. My mother would plotz if she really knew what I've been up to!

So tell me about Scott G. School is a bummer, it's so hard. The only thing I like about MWF is that I sit next to the cutest, sweetest hunkest best bod guy! I swear! I break out in a cold sweat everytime I look next to me.

Love ya Lou. Take it easy, but take it!

Love,

DIAL-A-GUILT-TRIP #1

Princess: Hi

Mother: What are you doing home on a Saturday night?

Princess: What are you doing calling on a Saturday night?

Mother: Your father was worried about you.

Princess: Well, I'm going to the ZBT Midnight Madness party.

Mother: 12 o'clock at night and you're first going out? I hope you're not walking there alone. Make sure you have a ride home.

Princess: Don't worry, I won't be coming home . . . I mean I'm sleeping at Brenda's dorm.

Mother: What are you wearing?

Princess: Well, I really have nothing good to wear because I've gained so much weight this semester. Nothing fits and I don't have any money to buy anything new.

Mother: If you didn't spend all your money ordering out for pizzas you wouldn't have either problem.

Princess: Listen, I gotta go. I'm late.

Mother: Just a minute! The reason I called is Bernice Firedman's son is in the AEPi house and . . .

Princess: You mean the tall one with zits? Forget it! I'll talk to you next week. Don't forget to tell daddy to deposit my allowance.

GREEK GLOSSARY

ACTIVE: A Princess who's finally been initiated into lifelong membership in AEPhi or SDT, and now only has to "actively" worry about finding a Prince.

ALUMNA: The Princess who's graduated from college but attends all sorority functions in an effort to cling to her youth.

BID NIGHT/BID TO PLEDGE: The time and act of officially inviting the Princess to join the sorority. Referred to as a bid because it's so similar to dealing in commodities.

CHAPTER HOUSE: Dilapidated structure on college campus housing girls the Alumni have never met but who are always asking for donations for repairs.

FORMAL RUSH: Referring to a period in time during which a Princess hurriedly learns to outdo all the 'competition by wearing a Givenchy evening gown.

INFORMAL RUSH: Same as above carried off in Blassport.

INITIATION: Rite in which sorority sisters dress up in sheets, perform strange ceremonies in the dead of the night in the sacred chapter room. One of the few times in her life the Princess will not be concerned about proper evening attire.

PLEDGE: A girl who's just joined a sorority. Not to be confused with promises made to donate a certain large sum of money to Pioneer Women.

LEGACY: The inherited birthright of every Princess to be a Princess. Also refers to a Princess who, no matter how creepy she is, is automatically given a bid because every single one of her relatives was in the house too.

QUOTA: Hearkening back to the times when there was a limit on the number of the Princess' refuge ancestors who could enter America. Now refers to the number of princesses the Theta's will accept in a decade.

COLLEGE SPORTS
Avoiding I.M. Sports

Intramural sports, the panacea of Prep, are the bane of the JAP's existance. Not for the Princess are dorm volleyball matches, touch football leagues and Spring baseball tournaments. Although I.M. sports provide good exercise and help establish camaraderie among dormmates, they simply involve too much risk for the Princess . . .

she could break a nail, ruin her hair or blow her nose job.

The only I.M. sport the Princess deems worthy of her participation is that of spectator. From the NJB's frat basketball games to their volleyball tournaments she is always the best dressed spectator on the sidelines.

Tennis — The Royal Sport

Although she shuns I.M. sports, the Princess does favor this elite game and, if she doesn't pick it up while in her teens or at college, she will undoubtably learn it later in life. Tennis etiquette for the Princess is as follows:

KNOW THE EQUIPMENT —

1. Wilson aluminum racquet and

2. Wilson balls (both recommended by the Pro)

3. Gucci ball bag and racquet cover (of course Vuitton may be substituted for both of the above, but never mix and match)

4. Spare make-up kit (you never know who you'll meet on the courts)

Once you've taken care of the basics, heed these adages and you'll be a winner both on and off the court. (A savvy Princess once needlepointed them onto her racquet cover)

"It's not whether you win or lose, but how you're dressed for the game."

"Winning isn't everything, it's the only thing, especially when it comes to getting the cutest Pro."

KNOW THE JARGON —

Set: Comprised of 6 games. Not to be confused with the same number of pieces in a Tiffany place setting.

Match: Six sets to a match and, as in real life, they are not always made in heaven.

Love: Love is *never* nothing to the Princess; she *always* knows score.

KNOW THE CLOTHES —

Proper attire for the Princess should include:

1. Filas warm-up suit

2. Fetching tennis dress with ruffly panties peeking out.

3. Peds with pom-poms

4. Tretorn shoes

5. No need for a sweatband, a Princess does *not* perspire.

Initial Reaction Quiz

1. It is acceptable to have your stationery engraved with "Mrs. Mark Hirsch, M.D."?

   A. True, if you're using it to write letters to women in your B'nai B'rith group.
   B. False, but whenever referring to your husband, refer to him as "Dr. Mark".

2. The initials "J.D." stand for Jewish Divorce.

   A. True, but don't give yourself any kenahoras.
   B. False, it means he's a lawyer and if he proposes, accept immediately.

3. D.D.S. is a feminine hygeine spray.

   A. True. but nice Jewish Princesses don't have to know from those.
   B. False, it's someone who knows the only time when gold-filled is acceptable.

4. CPA is Chicago's floundering transportation system.

   A. True, and Jane Byrne's real name was Joyce Bernstein and she had her nose bobbed and her hair bleached.
   B. False, and there's no accounting for not latching onto one of these money makers.

5. P.H.D. are the most desirable letters to appear with the name Bruce Mandel.

   A. True, he's a nuclear physicist no less.
   B. False, the most desirable letters to appear with *any name* are M.R.S., as in Mrs. Bruce Mandel.

Q. Why did the Princess put gold in her diaphragm?
A. She wanted her boyfriend to come into money.

It's a Matter of Degree — Continuing Education

If the Princess had been lucky in grades but unlucky in love, this is the time to consider graduate school. Name your professional — Doctor, Lawyer or MBA — all earn a good living. They might not be as carefree as undergrads, but what they are lacking now in social graces they will make up for later in future fortunes. And these guys are really serious about their future. The smart Princess will make damn sure that she's a part of it. They are so busy studying, that if you get in on the ground floor, they won't even have time to look for anyone else.

A dividend to post-grad study is the degree you'll be receiving. A smart Princess is a precious commodity and she'll never be alone for long. Always in demand for dinner parties with her clever conversation and witty repartee. And, who knows, since the

Princess is so used to getting her own way, she'll probably end up as chairman of the board!

The Princess knocked wearily on the door to yet another castle. It had been a long, lonely journey but she was nearing the end. She had trudged up and down endless flights of stairs, walked the never ending blocks of her new kingdom-to-be and rung countless doorbells.

With no good fairy Princesses to guide her the Princess had undertaken the arduous task of finding a new dwelling. Alas and alack, she had only her mother to rely on . . . a mother who insisted on an elevator building (with doorman), and peeked into the vegetable bins of refrigerators in every place they saw. And now, they were at their journey's end . . . "large convertible studio, new carpeting, Levelor blinds, wall-to-wall-carpeting, beautifully decorated, includes heat and A/C", the ad read. And so, the good fairies did again smile on the Princess (or was it her mother's checkbook?).

And thus a new chapter unfolds, the escapades of . . .

CHAPTER 4

The Great Escape

THE URBAN PRINCESS

*From the Lap of Luxury
to the Rehab Realm*

FROM THE LAP OF LUXURY TO THE REHAB REALM

A Princess can only sponge off her parents for so long. After college it's time to strike out on her own.

Equipped with a diploma and a diaphragm, the Princess moves into a cozy little studio apartment in the city hoping it will only be a short time until Prince Charming sweeps her off her feet. She chooses a geographically desirable location where she will be surrounded by others of her own ilk. No mingling with the peasants for the Princess . . . she has selected the area where all her friends live. Once ensconced, her phone number will be released to the local fix-up network. While she once scorned blind dates, she now welcomes them as the only way to meet anyone decent. And how can she miss? Only doctors and lawyers subscribe to this network and a dinner is a dinner.

Eventually all of this pays off and the Princess is ready to accept a suitable number of carats and start thinking of the suburbs.

DADDY'S LITTLE GIRL
Quotes from Escaped Princesses

When the Princess finally leaves the familial fortress for a high rise palace of her own, her father is careful to make sure that she is safe from sleazy swains and luring lancelots. His Princess must be guarded by knights in shining armour (aka, doormen). And the Princess must convince her frantic father that it is impossible to find a Manhattan apartment with a moat and a drawbridge, no matter how much he's willing to help out with the rent.

Here are a few quotes from some Princesses who've escaped (just barely):

"I saw my father parked outside my apartment for three straight days. Fearing he'd starve, I bought him a sandwich from the deli on the corner. He was thrilled to see I was learning to cook."
B. Stein, Scarsdale

"My father shlepped all my furniture up to my 5th floor walkup because he didn't want the movers to know that I was living alone."
K. Gold, Highland Park

"Two weeks after I moved in, my father, who is not spontaneous, dropped by at 3 a.m. saying he "just happened to be in the neighborhood." Rob almost suffocated in my closet!
R. Fine, Miami Beach

"Last winter when my car was buried under three feet of snow, daddy showed up with a shovel, only to come back two days later with the next snowfall. This time I had the schnapps ready."
Debbie L., Rogers Park

Royal Entendre

Princess Says	Princess Really Means
I love your new outfit	That was a second reduction at Saks
So your fiancee teaches school	She'll be shopping at Macy's
It's nice of you to make dinner for Sheldon again	Too bad he's too cheap to take you out
That's a beautiful setting for your engagement ring. Can I see it a little closer?	*How* could she accept less than a carat?
So you're visiting your parents over Winter break this year	Huh . . . she can't get a date for New Year's
I haven't seen you in that outfit in a long time	She gained back all her weight

POST-PALACE DECORATING

The Kitchen

1. Food Processor — the Princess doesn't know how to use it but it was a gift her mother got for depositing a certain sum in a new savings account (In the Princesses name no less!)

2. Waring Blender — for Weight Watcher shakes

3. Toaster Oven — instead of the oven, primarily used for melted-cheese-on bialy sandwiches.

4. Silverwear drawer — Full set of mother's old stainless and a variety of carry-out menus.

5. Sink — Holds dried silk flower arrangement.

6. Dishwasher — always filled with glasses

7. Contents of Cabinets — set of china left over from her first engagement, Corning Ware that's never been used

8. Oven — Used to store pots and pans (Princess will occasionally use the Teflon frying pan.)

9. Tupperware — Purchased at married friend's Tupperware party

10. Pantry — 6 cans of Geisha white tuna in water, diet iced tea mix, Bran cereal, Tam-Tams, 2 lb. bag of M&M's for company.

11. Refrigerator —
freezer: Weight Watcher Frozen Treats, 1 Empire Kosher chicken (welcome present from Grandma), Lean cuisine frozen dinners.
fridge: Tab, nail polish, white wine

12. Canister set — All empty except for Sugar which holds Sweet 'n Low

13. Under Sink — Tin foil, extra toweling paper, Ivory Liquid (for

washing pantyhose) paper plates, napkins from carry-out joint, paper cups.

14. Ceramic magnets in the shape of food holding diets, incentive pictures, lo-cal recipes, invitation to Sholom Singles Dance (unsolicited)

Note absence of phone — too dangerous to have in kitchen.

Main Room

15. Double bed with Hollywood cover

16. Rattan Chairs

17. Over stuffed Marimekko pillows

18. High Tech coffee table with candy dish of Barton's Diet Coffee Candy, bowl of matchbooks from everywhere she's been on a date.

19. Bong

20. Plant collection: Wandering Jew, spider plant, jade tree, Ficus tree, philodendron

The move to the city is a big step. It is the first (and probably the last) time the Princess will be alone and her first apartment is a long way from the comforts of her early Palace years at home. Having sworn off female roommates forever she looks forward to the privacy and lack of competition for the beaux she will now enjoy. But she will not lack a close confidant, however, for her best friend lives in an identical studio in the same building.

21. Issues of **Vogue** for the last 6 months

22. Framed poster of old deco Vogue cover

23. Glass and chrome etegere holding her collection of classics: The Complete Scarsdale Diet, Weight Watchers Cookbook, Marjorie Morningstar, Sheila Levine is Dead and Living in New York, Portraits, Collected Works of Phillip Roth, top 10 paperback best sellers, photo albums dating back to birth, backgammon, Uno, nude picture taken last year at Club Med.

24. Track Lights

25. Panasonic Stereo (Princesses are not technically inclined)

26. Color TV with remote control and Betamax

Bathroom

26. Fluffy toilet seat cover

27. matching rug

28. coordinated wastebasket, Kleenex box, soap dish and cup

29. Clairol light up Mirror-Mirror

30. Toothbrush-and-a-spare

31. Lens cooker, boil and soak solution

32. Glasses

33. Shower door — must be wiped down after every use

34. Bath mat stolen from Holiday Inn

35. Towels left over from college

36. Make-up counter from Saks

37. Perfume, Opium, Chloe, Bala Versailles, Halston, Chanel #19

38. Electric Rollers

39. Curling Iron

40. Blow Dryer

41. Rosamond Print

Rules for Sex

Now that you've determined a potential partner's suitability, and the next step is inevitable, be sure you handle yourself (and him) in a manner befitting a Princess.

Use protection. While the pill may make you feel fat and irritable, it's the safest, and perfect for spontaneous sex. But since Jewish girls are not spontaneous about anything, and will just *die* if they're gaining weight, the diaphragm is a better choice. *Get one and use it.* You know if you go for an abortion you'll never be able to lie well enough to your mother about why you missed two days of work.

Wear clean lingerie. You know what your mother always said about car accidents. Also be sure you've shaved your arms and legs. Sex with socks isn't the same.

Always be coy and make him spend a lot of money before you give in. Jewish girls equate money with love. The more he spends, the more he must love you.

Always have him at your place. You've practiced seductively draping yourself around your apartment. You know the sheets are clean. And you don't want to miss any phone calls.

Resist the urge to call your friends and tell them you've got someone there. It is permissable, however, if a friend calls you to intimate that you're being intimate and plan to see her later to discuss all the details.

Never say yes until you've made another date with him. There are many clever ways to do this. Like inviting him to your parents for dinner. Or inviting him on your roommate's parents' sail boat. (Note: **Do not** under any circumstances invite your new beau to a wedding or Bar Mitzvah, this is dangerous, especially if you want to see him again.)

ESSAY ON A _ _ _ _ _ _ S

This particular type of man really appeals to the Princess. The worse he treats her, the more she likes him. The Princess thrives on the anxiety of not knowing when, or even if, he'll call. When he does call, on a Friday night for Saturday, the Princess breathes a sigh of relief, knowing she'll be able to show-off her new outfit and manicure — if he shows up.

When he doesn't call, the Princess tells herself it's because he . . .

Doesn't use the phone on Shabbos

Is moving

Is busy with work and/or a client in town

Has a family function

Has friends of indeterminate gender in town

Is breaking up with his old girlfriend

Spends weekends with his kids from his first marriage

Is playing racquetball with the guys (don't even bother learning the game, because if you do, this excuse will become inexcusable.)

Had his car towed last week and it's probably still in the shop

Probably tried calling you, but since you haven't been home all week, he couldn't reach you and you never get your messages at work.

5 Reasons why he's with another woman

1. He only sleeps with her

2. His mother fixed him up with her

3. You were busy the one night he called (well, that one backfired)

4. She's a client

5. Don't send pictures of the last date you went on — that shows you in elephant bells and a poorboy sweater — even if it was with him.

Times When you can Convince Yourself it's OK to Call Him

1. When you've just deplaned, so you can show off your Carribean tan before you fade.

2. To return his left sock from the last time

3. If you haven't been home all week to receive his calls

4. When a "friend" of yours is in need of his professional services (i.e. doctor, lawyer)

5. To invite him to a wedding/Bar Mitzva/dinner party (make sure you've seen him in the last 2 weeks.)

Don't try these — even if you're desperate:

1. Ask him for dinner because you're afraid he isn't eating right.

2. Call him and say you just walked in and the phone was ringing and you thought it might be him (variation on theme — you were in a meeting and got a message that someone called and you thought it might be him.)

3. Don't leave your underwear behind at his apartment, he might return it at an inappropriate time.

Moral of the story: Nice Guys finish last with a Princess

JOBS FOR JAPS

#1
"I mean, in my dress I can't eat a thing. I'll just do lines all night."

#2
"Will there be anyone good there? I'll have to lay out all day."

#3
"Like, Josh drew the line at 300, so not everyone is invited with dates."

Copywriter on Madison Ave. M.A. from Medill. Looks like she's always dressed for a costume party.

Assistant Buyer at Bloomingdales. Career bride, fresh out of Sophie Newcomb. Favorite haunt is the bridal registry.

Lawyer with her father's firm. University of Miami grad. Prematurely wrinkled. Engaged to a dentist from Woodmere.

The Princess has a jump on the thousands of college grads entering the job market every June. The Jewish network has more jobs than the New York Times want ads. Her father and other MOTs (Members of the Tribe) can get her in the doors her resume can't. And, once she's in, she's there to stay, for who can say no to the bright and eager Princess?

The Princess is always a good employee because she loves to perform for an audience. For instance, the junior partners in the law firm, the Residents at the hospital, the assistant account executives at the advertising agency and especially the brokers on the commodities exchange. Obviously, to meet the right people, the Princess must have the right job.

Q. How can you tell if a Princess is having an orgasm?

A. She drops her nail file.

ALL OCCASION ORDERING OUT

The old adage says that the way to a man's heart is through his stomach. But since the princess possesses no culinary talents and doesn't want to take the chance of poisoning a "hot one", she becomes adept at choosing just the right carry out for the occásion.

The Princess knows the best pizza (thick or thin), ribs, chicken and Chinese in town that deliver. She knows just what to order and just what substitutions to make. She also knows all the places that take checks. Over-ordering is her forte. Many an affair has been consumated with cold Chinese out of the carton.

There comes a time when to-go from the deli won't do. The moment of truth always arrives and the Princess must be tested before saying "I do." That's why it's important to have one friend that really does know how to cook. She can then either teach the Princess a fool-proof recipe, or if even that is too risky, the Princess may be able to persuade her to do the cooking. The danger in this is if he asks you to make the same dish twice, but by then it will be too late.

Q: What do Princesses make for dinner?

A: Reservations.

The Perfect Prince

(Note subtle display of law diploma)

The Perfect Prince, every Princess' dream, is a knight, not in shining armor but a 3 piece suit (preferably pinstriped). Of course, a suit alone does not a Prince make. What about his tie? His briefcase? His shoes? His *father?!?*

Is he following in his father's footsteps? OK if his father is an investment banker but if he's merely a merchant your Prince will need his MBA, JD, CPA or MD to make him truly desirable. Of course, if he's a commodities broker the only degrees you need worry about are in the tropical spots he'll be taking you for weekend getaways.

Not only must he *look* like the Prince of your dreams but he must like the kinds of things you do as well. It's amazing how the thought of a baseball game on Saturday afternoon (when you could be hitting the sales) suddenly becomes attractive. Especially when you know the game will be followed by games more to your liking later in the evening (preceeded by dinner and a show, of course).

Because the Perfect Prince knows how to treat his Princess he will lavish gifts upon her and pay her the kind of attention she deserves . . . and demands.

Perfect Princely Personality Traits

1. Knows how long to hold out before calling, while at the same time letting you think you're on top of the situation (what you can't have is what you want most).

2. Is kind to your mother . . . eats her brisket on Friday, even has seconds then allows her to pack a care package. But, best of all, he calls her by her first name.

3. Can talk to your father . . . even about things *other* than sports.

4. Owns a condo in a luxury building with pool, sauna and exercise room . . . and he wouldn't *dream* of asking you to help with the assessments.

5. Has fine taste in clothes. Would never buy a fake suede jacket . . . much less wear one!

6. Wants you to meet *his* parents. This is when you know you've really hooked him.

THE
JEWISH AMERICAN PRINCESS
ON TELEVISION

Guest editorial
by: Sid Liebenson

The Jewish American Princess has been identified in literature for a generation already, thanks to Herman Wouk, Philip Roth, et al. She loves to read novels (only best sellers and an occasional saga . . . you know, up from Russia to the teeming lower east side to the penthouse apartments of Fifth Avenue and on to Hollywood). And there's nothing a Princess likes to read about more than others of her kind.

Which brings me to television. Why aren't there more Jewish Princesses on television? After all, if there's one thing a true JAP enjoys more than a good date, it's good TV. Ever since she got a 12 inch black and white for her Bat Mitzvah, television has been the Muzak of her life. At least one television is always on in the house . . . usually two, tuned to the same channel. This way she can go from the kitchen to the den without missing one line from Love Boat.

Or My Three Sons . . . or David Hartmann . . . or Phil Donahue. The Princess has an amazing appetite for television. She also has an amazing tolerance for pap. Like a friend of mine said, "If it's in color and it moves, I'll watch it!"

Many network seasons ago the Princess *was* rewarded with a television portrayal of herself. It was in the mid-to-late sixties when the greatest JAP show of them all hit the airwaves and girls all over America could watch their Princess dreams come alive when Marlo Thomas played "That Girl."

That Girl?! It was *perfect!* New York . . . glamour . . . rubbing shoulders with Broadway stars . . . being the girl *everybody* noticed. She even met her future husband in the *first* episode!

Jewish or not, Ann Marie personified the ideal Princess experience. After college she left her Westchester county home

(Brewster) to find fame and fortune in the city (New York no less!) And her first fortunate find was a cute but sizable one bedroom apartment in a charming brownstone, complete with friendly neighbors (most New Yorkers are lucky if they even *know* their neighbors). Of course, she lived in it all by herself and could afford it on a part-time actress' salary. Right? Come on now, we know better than that!

Every Princess can easily imagine scenes they didn't show on television:

Mom and dad scouting for apartments with Ann.

Dad nixing anything on First Avenue (too near the bars).

Mom nixing anything on Lexington (too tacky).

Everyone deciding that the big brownstone apartment was *perfect* for Ann.

Daddy's checkbook opening as he writes out the security deposit check and wonders at the outrageously high cost of city living.

Monthly checks coming directly from Lou Marie in Brewster.

Ah well, nothing's too good for his Princess.

And, of course, would-be actresses as well as Princesses need to be in the latest of fashion. So, every week, the TV audience was treated to the newest in New York styles and every real Princess knew in her heart that in Ann Marie's Coach bag was a Bloomingdale's credit card, *in her father's name.*

But clothes and a dress do not a perfect Princess make. Ann Marie also had ideal Princess conditions. Let's look at them individually:

1. An only child. Princess Ann grew up enjoying the full attention of doting parents. No brothers who might monopolize family pride. No sisters who might have better hair or bigger breasts and who would compete for daddy's attention. Everything she got was new and no one had to get it next. And what better way to prepare for being the focus of everyone in New York than growing up being the focus of daddy and mom.

2. Glamorous job. Being an unemployed actress may not seem like an exciting career but it sure beats working. You're always free to lunch with mom and you can get your shopping done when the stores aren't crowded. So, careerwise, Ann had it made. And, when she did work, she could meet famous people, go to exciting places and never worry about being bored. She was always in the spotlight . . . just like in the living room back home.

3. The Brewster homestead. A Westchester upbringing is a real plus in Princess life. Brewster may not be Scarsdale but, if you do your shopping in White Plains, it still qualifies as Princess breeding grounds. And, for a girl in New York, it had the added advantage of proximity. Daddy and mom are just a short commuter train ride away so it's easy to run home for the weekend, an evening or a seder dinner. It also means daddy or mom can run down to the city in case of emergency. Like when the refrigerator needs defrosting or when the overhead light has burned out.

4. Daddy's money. A prerequisite

for high Princessdom. Daddy should be considered "an unlimited source of funds," and, even if Ann never said those words, she probably thought of him that way. Even though Lou ran a restaurant he seemed to be doing OK and at least Ann never seemed to want for anything.

5. The boyfriend. Bright, witty, handsome, intelligent, Don Hollinger was all a Princess could ask for. He indulged Ann's every whim and joined in all the escapades but all the while acted as a stabilizing force to keep her in line (Good grief, just like daddy?). Don was older, a bit more worldly, but from out of town so Ann could be the New York expert. Better yet, Don's family was safely off in St. Louis so they could spend every holiday with *her* family.

Still, there were a few elements in Ann Marie's life that were just slightly less than perfect for a Princess. Let's start with the name. Come on now! No self respecting Princess would have Marie for a first name, much less a last name. And there's daddy's business. Restaurant supply would be more like it. With just a restaurant (not even a chain) what's the likelihood of ever hiring Don into the business?

Finally, there's Don's job. In any position even slightly related to journalism there's too great a danger of relocation. A professional man would be better. At least you can count on his staying in New York. Even a stockbroker. Or at least someone who could be hired into daddy's (or his own dad's) business. The "Newsview" job doesn't even have snob appeal. That may have been the main

reason Ann waited so long to marry him.

But marry Don she did, even if it took five television seasons. But, when you can run home to daddy's money or to hide under mom's bed, who's in any rush? Anyway, by the early Seventies Ann was in hotpants and going braless so it was probably Don who forced the question.

Where are they now? Brewster, if Ann got her way (and what Princess doesn't?) OK, maybe even Scarsdale. Lou finally talked Don into joining the "Club" and they've even learned to enjoy their Sunday morning golf games together. Ann meets mom for lunch and shopping every Wednesday and on Saturdays, Ann and Don drop their J-named kids (Jennifer, Jessica, Jamie, Jason, Joshua, Jeremy or Jarrett) off with her parents so they can get some time alone.

So for every Princess who ever looked into a Madison Avenue shop window and saw herself in a bridal gown waving back, or even imagined herself strolling with a parasol among the show posters at Lincoln Center, there will always be the one TV show that brought the Jewish Princess dream to reality playing somewhere in syndication . . . That Girl!

Editor's note:
Mr. Liebenson is alive and well and living in Chicago where he keeps a disc antenna atop his house in his endless search for reruns of That Girl. He has been in intensive analysis for the past two years, ever since Marlo Thomas married Phil Donahue.

DIAL-A-GUILT-TRIP #2

Princess: Hello

Mother: Where have you been all nite?

Princess: It's only 6:30!

Mother: Were you going to call me?

Princess: I still have my coat on!

Mother: Her own apartment for two months and she thinks she's a big shot!

Princess: Oy (sigh) mother, did you call for a special reason?

Mother: Does a mother *need* a reason to call?

Princess: How's daddy?

Mother: If you ever called here you wouldn't have to ask a question like that!

Princess: So, how are you feeling?

Mother: Why, you aren't worried are you?

Princess: No mother

Mother: So, why aren't you worried?

Princess: Listen, mother I've got to go, I'm being picked up in 10 minutes

Mother: You have a date? What does his father do?

Princess: I don't know, mom.

Mother: Oy, now she's going out with strangers!

Princess: I gotta go, he's honking

Mother: What kind of gentleman is he, he can't even come to the door!

Princess: GOODBYE mother, I'll call you tomorrow

Q. What is a Princess' favorite wine (whine)?
A. "I wanna go to Miami!"

Keeping the Princess in Style

The Princess loves to give and receive gifts . . . no occasion is too insignificant to remember. She will spend the hours she could be reading the latest trash novel cruising Loehmann's searching for the perfect sentimental gift and she expects no less in return. She will drop none-too-subtle hints including size and style numbers to make sure she gets what she wants.

Unfortunately, the signals between she and her Prince often cross but the Princess believes it is better to have received and returned than to never have received at all.

Occasion	Gift Prince Thinks is Appropriate	Gift Princess Expects
Birthday	Candy	Diamond Earrings
Anniversary	Flowers	Diamond eternity ring
Hannukah	Subscription to McCalls magazine	8 gold bracelets
Sweet 16	Keys to dad's car	Firebird
Bat Mitzvah	Trip to grandma's Miami condo	Trip to Israel
Valentine's Day	One rose in bud vase	Two dozen roses
Sweetest Day	Fruit & nut assortment	Godiva chocolates
Mother's Day	Parachute nylon luggage	Bottega Veneta bag
Saturday	½ off Plitt tickets	Theater tickets
Rainy day	Umbrella	Week in Acapulco
Job Promotion	Commuter bus pass	Gucci briefcase
Housewarming	Dustbuster	Baccarat crystal vase
Sick day	Cough medicine	Dior silk nightgown
Break a nail	Valium	1 oz. Flacon Opium perfume

AFTER HOURS AVAILABILITY

Los Angeles

Monday   **Hamburger Hamlet** Brentwood, San Vicente Blvd. Princesses feast first then work off your calories with dancing at this fun, young spot.

Tuesday   **The Red Onion,** Marina Del Rey. Hangout here for fabulous fun. The young professionals frequent this spot for its outdoor garden in back.

Wednesday   **Rodeo Drive** and then **The Ginger Man,** Beverly Hills, Bedford Drive. Get in some quick shopping at the Glamorous boutiques then drive up to the Ginger Man in a yellow Rolls Royce or a Red Ferrari fit for a Princess. Have a drink or two and maybe even a late supper.

Thursday   **Morton's** and then **Trump's,** West Hollywood, Melrose. Transplanted Princesses love having dinner at Morton's...opened by the son of Chicago's favorite restauranteur, Arnie Morton. Wind up the evening with an after dinner drink at Trump's.

Friday   **Moustache,** Westwood, on Brockton. Live dangerously and endulge in wonderful chocolate mousse at this spot favored by Princesses from UCLA. Then spend the rest of the night, and maybe even part of the next morning at **The China Bar** in West Hollywood on Melrose.

Saturday   After a day of tanning at **Venice Beach** hit the hot spots around town. First to **El Pravado** on Sunset Blvd. for disco then finish up **after** hours at **Sneaky Pete's.** In-the-know Princesses will know how to find it.

Sunday   **Marina Del Rey.** Clever California Princesses will have an invitation for sun and fun by this time. Sail from the Marina on the yacht of some movie mavin.

Chicago

Monday   **Mel Markon's** in the heart of Lincoln Park. Lots of lo-cal entrees, good place to start diet after weekend.

Tuesday   **La Relais** for cocktails, outdoor cafe a good place to see and be seen on Chicago's chicest street.

Wednesday	Princesses don't eat on this night in Chicago; **Loehmann's** is open late. Best to go with your mother.
Thursday	**East Bank Club.** Where the chic sweat. Last chance for a Sat. nite date. Restaurant mem- bership not half as desireable as full membership.
Friday	**Pump Room** for free hors d'ouvres in this world-famous room. Next hit **The Beau- mont** (it's the Jewish singles bar). You'll see everyone you've ever known.
Saturday	**Esquire** for good first run movies. **Morton's** for steak (if he takes you here, he's good for a second date).
Sunday	**Faces,** for Sholom Singles nite. This hot spot is taken over by 200 MOTs looking for mates. You don't have to know anyone to get in, only be desperate.

Washington D.C.

Monday	**Deja Vu,** 21st & "M" Streets. It's hard to tell the Princesses from the Preppys at this after work spot.
Tuesday	**Pierce Street Annex,** 19th Street. Another spot for making your- self available after hours. Have a glass of white wine and size up the lawyers and politicians.

Wednesday	**White Flint Mall,** Rockville, Md. Don't schedule any meetings after 5 p.m. and allow yourself plenty of time to make it here for some serious shopping to get ready for the weekend.
Thursday	**Sign of the Whale,** 1825 "M" Street. It's almost Friday . . . getting late if you don't have a date. Find a fellow Princess and stop here for happy hour and happy hunting.
Friday	**Rumors** 19th Street. Good spot for Princess- es on the prowl . . . or even come with a date if you're lucky enough to have one.
Saturday	**The 3rd Edition,** 1218 Wisconsin Ave., N.W. Have your Prince bring you here for a Royal dinner.
Sunday	**Georgetown.** Spend Sunday afternoons and early evening strolling around this area with your Prince. See if you can talk him into buying you dinner at one of the many quaint restaurants here.

New York

Monday	**Maxwell's Plum,** 64th St. and 1st Avenue. If you don't know this one, where have you been hiding? Actually great for Princesses any night of the week. Might as well get started early.
Tuesday	**One Fifth,** 1 Fifth

Avenue. This really elegant place for drinking, dining and listening to great music is always a favorite with the downtown Princess.

Wednesday   **New York Health and Racket Club,** all over Manhattan. Great place to play . . . all kinds of games. Fun for Princesses looking for a partner on the courts and off.

Thursday   **Shelter,** 540 2nd Avenue. For the upper East side Princess on her way up. Don't forget to ask if he's got a "share." Could mean fun weekends in the Hamptons. If you have no luck here, try **GRASS** at 1445 1st Ave. for the same kind of action.

Friday   **Ruelles,** 321 Columbus Avenue. Move to the chick West Side on Weekends. Princesses have recently discovered this side of town.

Saturday   **The Red Parrot,** 617 W. 57th St., for dancing 'till dawn. If you lose a Maud Frizon slipper on the way out, your Prince just **may** return it.

Sunday   **Peppermint Park,** 2nd Avenue. End the weekend right and swap stories about your perspective Prince over giant scoops of chocolate Chocolate Chip at this East Side ice cream parlor.

Miami

Monday   **Ginger Man,** at Mayfair on Coconut Grove. No retiring Princesses retire here after work. Great place to pick up a potential Prince.

Tuesday   **Cy's,** Rivergate Plaza, Brickle Avenue. Young professionals congregate here. Drinking and dining in the high income district of Miami.

Wednesday   **Sportsrooms.** All over South Florida Princesses meet at these deluxe spas to get in shape for the weekend and to shape up their weekend by meeting a man.

Thursday   **Turnberry Isle Disco,** Biscayne Blvd. Things don't start happening until almost midnight at this chic, members only spot in North Miami Beach. Any Princess who's anyone wouldn't miss Thursday night here.

Friday   **The Cricket Club,** Biscayne Blvd. Another exclusive key club where beautiful Royalty (Princes and Princesses) dine and dance until the wee hours of the morning.

Saturday   **The Grove Isle Club,** on Grove Island, Coconut Grove. If you've made it here you've really made it.

One fine day the Princess was summoned by a knock at the door. As she opened it an armload of boxes from the three Bs . . . Bloomies, Bendel's and Bergdorf's were unceremoniously dumped in the vestibule. 'Oh no, where am I going to put these!", she cried in dismay. "I still haven't unwrapped yesterday's shipment from Saks." She looked around her chamber. The closets were overflowing. Her drawers were filled to the brim. On every available inch of floor space were stacked still more trinkets. "This has got to stop," she cried, "I'm shopping myself out of house and home!"

But even as she spoke there was another knock at the door. "This was just what I've been waiting for!", she exclaimed as she ripped off the cover and planted a kiss on a startled frog.

But alas and alack, nothing happened. The Princess knew it was time to peruse the boutiques and shopping malls in faraway lands from whence her Prince would come. But that's another story.

The moral of this story:
Try it before you buy it.

CHAPTER 5

The Designer Dictate

DRESSING
FOR SUCCESS

From Clothes to Nose

BODY TYPES

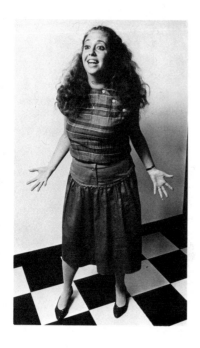

"I'll start again on Monday."

"I met this great guy. You'll love him, he's a lawyer."

No matter what shape the Princess comes in she's never satisfied. She's forever saying, "Five more pounds . . . " Still, there are two distinct Princess body types.

ZAFTIG PRINCESS

The zaftig Princess from the neck down bears a remarkable resemblance to a Rumanian peasant. Resting atop chicken legs and a flat **tush** are a Rubenesque belly and bosom. A zaftig Princess wears mostly black and hears a lot of "but she has such a pretty face."

SVELTE PRINCESS

The svelte Princess is built like her little brother from the waist up and like the side of a barn from the waist down. Consequently, she is always seen wearing skirts or harem pants that compliment her slim ankles and trim feet. The svelte Princess also owns tons of tiny tops and beautiful shoes.

Plastic Surgery Do's and Dont's

Plastic surgery before and after

DO

1. Choose a surgeon who has a good reputation among other Jewish Princesses.

2. Specify small nostrils.

3. Schedule your surgery at least 5 months before suntan season. Your new nose will look even cuter with a tan.

4. Plan on a two-week recovery period so no one has to see you black and blue. They'll think you look "rested" and plastic surgery will never cross their minds.

5. Have your eyebrows waxed immediately before surgery as you will not be able to tweeze them for several weeks (and who wants one straight-across eyebrow obliterating their new nose).

DONT

Choose a surgeon out of the phone book or one recommended by your friend Muffy Hicks-Smith.

Leave the decision about nostril size to your surgeon's discretion.

Go in for surgery during the Summer. Sunbathing can cause your new nose to swell and if you are pale, no one will notice your new nose anyway.

Have your nose done as an out-patient. Go for broke . . . insurance won't cover it anyway and you'll get lots of cute nightgowns and a mum plant arrangement with a band-aid across the nose.

Decide to go in for the natural look. After all, why are you having plastic surgery anyway?

FROM HAIR TO ETERNITY

The bane of the Princess' existence is her hair. Its set sets her mood for the day. At any given moment the Princess knows the relative indoor and outdoor humidity counts, her frizz is a more accurate gauge than the national weather service.

She learns to schedule all her activities around her hair. To a Princess, spontaniety means 2 hours from bathing through blow-drying, and foregoing the electric rollers.

Before the advent of Kindness rollers and Conair dryers, a Princess spent hour after hour with her hair wrapped around orange juice cans, attached to a bonnet hair dryer (All the vitamin C giving her the stamina to endure the prolonged baking.) In that bygone era, a flip that flopped was a fate worse than death.

Then a new wave appeared on the hair front and had frizzy-haired Princesses booking appointments weeks in advance. This was a chemical process called hair straigtening. Even though the ends of her hair split, it gave the Princess a reasonable facsimile of shiny and sleek.

Liberation finally came after years of wrapping and rolling — the "natural" became chic. While the *shiksas* were out perming theirs, the Princesses were regalling in masses of their own God given curls.

This freedom to frizz still left many Princesses unable to abandon their blow dryers, curling irons and hot combs, however. There are still thousands of Princesses who everyday engage in combat with their curls. And so it goes . . . from hair to eternity.

Q. What is the definition of a Princess nymphomaniac?

A. One who only has sex on days she gets her hair done.

Combat Tactics for the Hair-ied Princess

1. Everynight, sleep with your hair on top of your head in a soft headband (you should always wear this style when you are alone). One reason Princesses are virgins for so long is because they cannot sacrifice a night of wantonness for a day of waves.

2. Always carry an emergency hair kit in your purse. It should contain a soft headband, large and small barettes, ponytail holders and hair pins (This will get you out of more tight spots than your diagphram will.)

3. When en route anywhere, wear a "traveling hairdo." This involves putting your hair up in a manner in which it will make the least contact with the elements. (As this is impossible to do when going on a date, make sure he picks you up at your door, so he can see you pre-weather.)

4. Never make dates to go somewhere your hair might meet up with any moisture. This eliminates most sports and most other outdoor activities. If you happen to have a date and it rains, reschedule. It's better to cancel than to worry about your hair all night.

5. Plan a winter wedding. If you must have a suntan, go to Florida the week before.

Testimonial from a Former Frizzie

The happiest day of my life was the first time I got my hair straightened. Up at dawn, I went to La Femme in the Stevens Building where all the other North Shore Jewish girls went to be defrizzed. To this day, I remember sitting patiently for hours while Mildred performed miracles with the straightening solution. Then came 3 hours under the hairdryer, wrapping first one side of my hair, then the other. 8 hours later, voila! I could give any shiksa a run for her money — and that was with my old nose!

Debbie L., Rogers Park

THE PURSUIT OF THE PERFECT SUNTAN

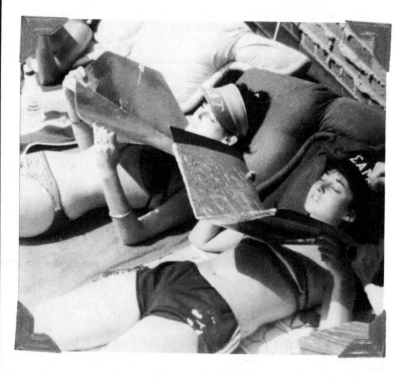

It is the unalienable right of every Princess to have a perfect tan. When the mercury hits 65° the pursuit begins in earnest. Armed with a reflector, Bain de Soleil with a 15 spf, DeepTan with an 8 spf, nosekote, funny plastic eyeshades and the latest from Harold Robbins, the Princess is ready for the ritual that will last until the first freeze. Princesses who are lucky enough to have that Mediterranean olive skin will be beautifully bronzed by the end of the weekend. Burning and peeling will not deter a Princess. She considers this an essential first step in her quest for the quintessential tan.

Rules for the Sun

1. Always take straps down. Strap marks look tacky, they **don't** show how dark you've already become.
2. Always cover your eyes — you'll probably need an eye lift, but why get it any sooner than absolutely necessary?
3. Use a sun block on your nose. Delicate tissues here have already been traumatized enough. (Those that have had one know what we mean.)
4. Keep a plant mister filled with cold water within easy reach. It will keep you cool and the water reflects the sun.
5. Wrap your book in tinfoil so that it, too, acts as a reflector.
6. Never eat while you are in the sun. You can sweat off up to 5 pounds and be svelte as well as suntan.

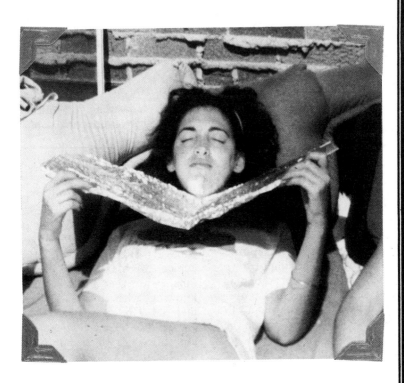

Getting in Style and Staying There

A Princess is never confused when confronted with a seemingly endless variety of fashion for sale. Never tricked by tacky trends, she adheres to these five tenets of Princess Purchasing:

1.	**Basic Black:**	Aside from being slenderizing, black is sophisticated, particularly in summer. Black is best from sun up to sun down, but skip it for evening clothes.
2.	**Fabulous Fads:**	Princesses are the first to adopt a look. If it's new they love it. For them classics are a non sequitur. Wear a fad until the copies come out.
3.	**Borrowed Clothes:**	What's in your roommate's closet always looks better than what's in your own. Borrow from your mother, too, even if she's not your size.
4.	**Overdressing:**	Not always in good taste, but always de rigeur. The trick is to get dressed and then add one more accessory. Then throw a few more in your purse "just in case" when you get there.
5.	**Initials**	Never your own. However, you must never, under any circumstances mix your monikers.

Dressing for Success — From Toddler to Trousseau

A Princess is born with shopping in her blood. Her earliest memories are of endless hours spent in the K.I.D.S. department of Saks donning outfit after outfit. Soon she starts asserting her own tastes and pre-school shopping sprees result in raging battles over whether it will be jeans and a "T" or ruffles and lace. Of course the savvy Princess knows she'll get away with getting both.

As the years pass the Princess refines her shopping skills to a high art form and she creates an image that's all her own. It is this sense of style, which encompasses everything from clothes to nose, which makes the Princess a formidable opponent indeed.

Knowing where to find the best buys in silk blouses, designer shoes at a discount and line by line copies of Maximillion furs is innate to the Princess. And knowing what to do with the material God gave her is, of course, her greatest talent . . . knowing what, where and when to nip, tuck and bob with discretion.

But never does her finesse shine brighter or pay off more than on that day she wears the gown she has so painstakingly selected . . . the gown she will wear only once, her wedding gown.

DRESSES

Worn mostly on special occasions, particularly nuptial affairs. If not an expensive silk, then the wider the better. Shopping for a dress is a painstaking process so allow plenty of time for perusing the stores. (Note: You may even have to resort to *retail.*)

1. **Trendy Dress:** Hides a multitude of sins. Looks up-to-the-minute as well.

2. **Mini-dress:** If you can carry it off wear this one when you want to make an entrance. If the Princess has skinny legs she can pair her mini with bright tights and bold accessories.

3. **Silk Dress:** Wardrobe staple. Good for business functions as well as weddings. Exudes an air of success.

4. **Knit Dress:** Not a clingy knit but a bulky one. Appropriate for temple wear and, with a jacket over it, for job interviews.

5. **Old Bridesmaid Dress:** Pseudo-chic in unflattering styles. Makes great Halloween costume . . . fun to dress up your date in them.

6. **Wedding Gown:** Self-explanatory.

TOPS

Easier to shop for than bottoms. The Princess can turn one top into dozens of new looks without once looking into a full length mirror. Mohair, metallic, cotton and silk are the fabrics chosen as the foil for her jewels.

1. **Adrienne Vitadini Sweaters:** In cotton, wool and silk, a wardrobe staple. The closest to a classic.

2. **Perry Ellis ruffled Blouses:** The essence of Princess-dom. Very expensive and out of style in a season.

3. **Hand Knit Metallic Sweater:** Big this season. Buy one (or better yet, have someone knit one for you) and everyone will think you're rich. Bulky yarns are good for hiding figure flaws.

4. **Silk Blouses:** Own them in every color of the rainbow. Go from office to on-the-town.

7. **Club Med T-shirt:** Brought back by boyfriend who had to go there to get laid (Princess is holding out for a ring).

8. **"Fat" Top** A *must* for post binge days. As those days are usually numerous, have several. Buy them on your skinny days for an ego boost.

BOTTOMS

A real trauma to shop for these. The waists are always too tight. The hemlines always too long. When a Princess finally finds a style that fits she should get them in every color.

1. **Sasson Jeans:** *We* don't wear them much anymore, but *we* were the ones who made them famous.

2. **"Fat" Pants:** For post binge days, wear with a "fat" top.

3. **Divided Skirt:** As trendy as it is practical, a new phenomenon for the Princess.

4. **Lee Jeans:** Cut fuller in the seat and the legs (just like the Princess) than Levis. Usually left over from college, can be dressed up or down.

5. **A-Line Skirt:** Neatly camouflages too much tush.

6. **Knickers:** Trendy but a Princess can get away with them at the office. Save them when a season is over . . . they've been making a comeback every 5 years.

7. **Wool Gab Slacks:** Always pleated, this style is flattering to all figure types. Wear them anywhere. Pair them with sandals and silk or a sweater and boots. Collect them in every color.

SHOES

The Jewish Princess is no barefoot Contessa but just *any* shoe won't do. The higher the heel the better; they're also more flattering to thick calves and short legs. Comfort is secondary when using the shoe as a status symbol. And finally, a Princess can *never* have too many shoes.

1. **Bandolinos:** Assorted styles. Make sure you have at least one pump. Look expensive. Eases transition from college to work.

2. **Charles Jourdan Slingbacks:** Look expensive because they are. Wear these and you can get away with last year's cocktail dress.

3. **Joan & David Flats:** What Bass is to Preps, J&D is to Japs. This year metallics are big.

4. **Ann Klein Pumps:** Dressy look from an M.O.T. Go gracefully from A.M. to P.M.

5. **Furry Slippers:** The ultimate leisure shoe . The rattier the better. Wardrobe staple, lasts for years. Comfortable respite from all those too-tall, too-tight shoes.

6. **Hana Mackler Boots:** Good leather boots for fashion, not function. Ideal for grabbing cabs in cold weather.

7. **Anything-but-Frye Boots:** Perfect with the new Prairie Look. Princesses simply *have* to be trendier than Frye.

8. **Peu-de-soie Pumps:** Dyed to match can be redyed for each bridesmaid dress.

9. **High Fashion Shoe:** Maude Frizon, Walter Steiger, Andrew Pfister. Beautiful leathers and highly styled, these way out looks put the Princess way ahead of the crowd.

COATS

A nice coat is essential for that all-important first impression. Make yours say JAP a mile off. To hold your own at twenty paces own . . .

1. **Slicker:** This one is always in for keeping the humidity out. Choose one with a visor hood. Keep a spare in the back seat of your Firebird.

2. **Cotton Jacket:** Sporty look for spring and summer. Because there's no hood, it's only worn when there is no rain in the forecast.

3. **Good Wool Coat:** Calvin Klein, Nipon or Trigere. Good for a professional image or when it's too risky to check your fur.

4. **Down Jacket:** Not to be confused with a ski jacket. For outdoor sports like window shopping and hailing cabs.

5. **Trendy Trench:** Luba. High styling belies its durability. Less dowdy than a classic Trench and equally as practical.

6. **Fur:** The ultimate in outerwear for the Princess. Cover casual or formal wear with your favorite endangered species.

7. **Suede Blazer:** Turns a skirt and blouse into a look, and pants into a suit. Can be worn year around. Over for Fall days, under for Winter. A Princess' answer to the navy blazer.

8. **Leather Jacket:** Sporty, in-between look. Goes with the interiors of Mercedes, Porsche or Jab.

GEAR

These garments round out the Princess' wardrobe. Stolen from her more active sister, the goyish prep, the Princess adopts this garb with a style no one else could hope to achieve.

1. **Millskin Leotard:** Worn with matching tights at the health club (i.e. pick-up spot par excellent). Accessorized with waterproof jewelry.

2. **Maillot Bathing Suit:** High cut leg to minimize thighs. Get one with a coordinated cover up, neither of which ever gets wet.

3. **Warm Up Suit:** This is for the Princess who only wants to *look* active. Also called a jogging suit when worn for running errands.

4. **Tennis Dress:** These are actually worn for sport so it's necessary to own several.

5. **Norma Kamali Sweatshirt Outfit:** Princesses love this hot new designer because she does not dress devotees of the Preppy Handbook.

NOTHING COMES BETWEEN LOUIS AND ME

Contents of the Princess' Purse

1, Louis Vuitton Purse

2. Louis Vuitton wallet and checkbook cover (with flowered checks)

3. Louis Vuitton eyeglass case. Designer glasses . . . can't see out of them but they look Devo.

4. Contact case

5. Make-up bag. Princess Borghese blush, bronzer, eye shadow, mascara, Clinique toner, skin medicine, 4 lipsticks, lip brush, travel curling iron, hairspray, ponytail holders, barettes, combs and soft headbands.

6. Gucci key ring.

7. Nail polish and emery board

8. Velamints (2 packs)

9. Old receipts, theater tickets, dry cleaning tickets.

10. Purse-size perfume spray, Chanel 19 Cross pen with flannel holder.

11. Assorted business cards. From all the friends and guys she meets in bars.

The Care and Feeding of a Fur

What a cloth coat is to a Republican, a fur coat is to a Princess. It conveys a sense of style and panache. Put one on, and she is regal. The confidence it gives her is worth forgoing taxis, leisurely lunches, the cleaning lady and her penchant for drycleaning everything.

Lest you think the Princess must always scrimp and save to pay for her fur, think again. The Princess relies on her wails as well as her wiles. A few well-paced hints to daddy about the freezing temps peppered with a cough and a sniffle . . . a few dropped hints to mother about how a doctor doesn't want a sickly wife and the Princess will be swathed in sable before the next snowfall.

Shopping for a fur isn't as difficult as it may seem. The Princess's earliest memories are of her mother cooing over her crib, "full skins, full skins." This eliminates fox pieces, muskrat paws, bunny fur and mouton lamb. Still the possibilities are numerous; raccoon, lynx, coyote, sheared beaver, fisher, and mink to name a few.

When a Princess dons a fur, she dons an attitude as well. A fur-clad Princess exudes a self assurance guaranteed to attract if not a Rothschild, at least a reasonable facsimile. Here too, the Princess ascribes to still another adage — money goes to money. What's more, it's one less gift the Prince will have to bestow on his Princess.

Forbidden Furs

Squirrel: Bright-eyed, bushy tailed and tacky, tacky, tacky. You'd be nuts to invest in one.

Rabbit Coats and Bunny Jackets: Don't hop too quickly to buy one of these. None too luxurious . . . this fur molts.

Fox Pieces: You can never be sure who's wearing the rest of your fur.

Mouton or Persian Lamb: Tres dreck! Who wants to wear a coat that might have been sewn by one of the Ayatolla's cousins?

The Princess' Guide to Choosing a Fur

Beaver: Looks good on all figures. If you're a little zaftig, a sheared beaver in a neutral color looks best.

Coyote: Looks best on the tall, thin Princess. Expensive, but the wild wanton look is worth every penny.

Curly lamb: Starter fur, popular on college campuses.

Fisher: Coming into its own, if you can afford to own it. For trendsetting Princesses.

Lynx: Luxurious long haired fur for the self indulgent Princess.

Mink: For the over-30 Princess. It announces you've arrived.

Muskrat: The look of a beaver at a fraction of the price.

Raccoon: Internationally identifiable symbol for a Princess. Looks lux on all of them.

Sable: Sure sign of success. Usually not acquired till after age 40.

Midwest winters drove me mad! Couldn't my ancestors have gotten off the boat in Miami? The only way I could possibly be warm was to wrap myself in fur. We're talking full skins for a poor working girl. After saving for two years I was still thousands short of my goal. I simply couldn't face another winter without a fur. As far as I could see the only solution was to sell something. You guessed it . . . I sold my car. My dad financed the remainder of this venture, and alighting from a cab in raccoon is ever so much more chic than pulling away from the curb in a Vega.

Myra B.,
Scarsdale

THE CROWN JEWELS

Diamonds are a Princess' best friend — as are sapphires, rubies, emeralds and all else that shines. The Princess is purely 14K. She'll wear anything that glitters as long as it's gold.

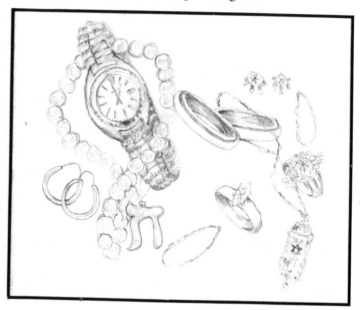

1. Rolex Watch
2. Diamond Stud Earrings
3. Engagement Ring
4. Pearls
5. Gold Earrings
6. Chi Necklace
7. Mezuzzah (this may be in silver)
8. Gold Chain Bracelets
9. Bangle Bracelets
10. Ring with big stones
11. Ankle Bracelet

The Scarsdale Diet as a Way of Life

Is there a Princess alive who hasn't slivered a Sarah Lee cheesecake to death? Those with willpower can at least claim that they've waited for it to thaw before devouring it.

For the Princess dieting is a way of life. Every last one of them can tell you the calorie counts in everything from a small salad (55 with 1 tablespoon of diet dressing) to a Snickers Bar (240, but worth every one). They spend a good part of every meal totaling and retotaling their calorie consumption for the day and have devised ingenious ways to get around these sneaky caloric units. And when they do cheat — they do it in a big way — the only way befitting a Princess.

lbs.
The Art of Cheating

The Pre-diet Pig Out —

It's Sunday night. Tommorrow is D- (diet) Day and you must rid yourself of all the goodies in your apartment so they won't tempt you during the week. The only solution is to eat every last Oreo, Frito, pint of Haagan Daas, slice of cold pizza and toasted bagel with the last scraping of cream cheese that you can lay your hands on.

This "pig-out" session is good for 3-5 lbs. but don't worry . . . you'll lose it by the second day of dieting and this pseudo weight loss will provide the incentive to stay on your diet until the next time your cupboard needs cleaning.

The Will Power Short Circuit —

You've been great on Scarsdale for a week. Not one granule of sugar or a single carbohydrate has passed your lips. It's Friday and you've already lost 5 lbs. this week so . . . on your way past the corner drug-store, when you hear a chorus of Snickers bars calling your name . . .

you go for it. It's only 240 calories . . . if you can stop at just one.

The Royal Cheat —

When you're ready to break your diet: Peanut butter & Fritos, Smuckers Strawberry Preserves & Super Chunk Skippy on a spoon, Chocolate Cheesecake with choc-olate chip Haagen Daas & Elmer's Goldbrick, any cheese on a bagel melted in the toaster oven or half dozen Snickers bars.

Menu Madness —

You have a date with a new beau and he takes you to an expensive Italian restaurant. You've ordered a low-cal glass of white wine but how can you impress him by passing on the pasta? As you signal the waiter for another bas-ket of garlic bread you suddenly remember you're on Weight Watchers. OK, you'll order Scampi (and cheese IS allowed). So enjoy. You're going to pay tomorrow but who can watch their weight when on a date?

SHOPPING —
WHOLESALE VS. RETAIL

Armed with an array of charge cards, shopping should be an effortless task for the Princess. This just isn't so. There looms before the Princess that great debate — wholesale vs. retail. On an unlimited budget any Princess can be well turned out, but buying on limited funds is the true test of her shopping prowess. Rich or not-so-rich, the Princess loves a bargain.

It's worth it to shlepp all the way down to Orchard Street to Aunt Fannie's friend the furrier for a good deal. Or to spend an entire day pawing through the racks at Loehmann's. When the Princess has succeeded in depleting the stock at discount prices or when she wants an outfit that still has the label sewn in, then she resorts to retail. Fifth Avenue and Fifty Seventh Street stores have their appeal.

Following is a list of where the Princess can leave her money from coast to coast.

Henri Bendels:
57th Street, NYC. Originator of the avant-garde window display. And what's inside is even better. The first floor is a haven for hats and other accessories.

Bergdorf's:
5th Avenue, NYC. Mecca for the more mature Princess. Introduction to this store comes with first foray into bridal salon. Great sales on designer ready-to-wear.

Bloomingdales:
59th and Lexington, NYC. This store is really the ultimate. If you can't find it at Bloomies, it just doesn't exist. Princesses receive their first Bloomies charge card at birth. (Note: Best place for bridal registry.)

Bonwit Teller:
57th Street. Branches in Boston, Chicago, etc. Main store closed for one year. Hasn't quite recaptured former glory, but still the best place to shop for lingerie and Hermes. Also magnificent Missoni Boutique and S'fari is a designer delight.

Burdines:
Fla. Sunbelt Bloomies.

Marshall Field & Co:
State Street, Chicago, also suburban locations in Illinois and the Galleria in Houston, TX. The Bloomies of the midwest. Noted for the bridal registry and return policy. They'll take it back even if you didn't buy it there.

Gumps:
San Francisco

I. Magnin:
San Francisco, Michigan Ave, Chicago. Famous for its Fur Salon especially in Chicago with Carol and Irwin Ware. Small but select assortment of designer fashions.

Neiman Marcus:
Houston and every other city where enough Japs live to warrant

opening one. Their Christmas catalog is a Princess' idea of mail order.

Saks Fifth Avenue:
Fifth Avenue, NYC. Great children's department ensures early initiation. A store with status. They put their own labels on everything and call it their own. Check out the merchandise here before you buy it wholesale.

Handmoor:
Adams Street, Chicago. One of the first discount designer outlets and the best bargain shopping in town. Princesses come from all over the Midwest. 20% off on all designer clothes. Be nice to the pushy salesladies, they're your ticket to rummaging through the racks and finding the real find. Great pre-season coat sale, great accessories and Meyers bags at a discount. Best of all, it looks like you paid retail.

Deciphering a Loehmann's Label

Loehmann's — the ultimate in designer mark-downs is much, much more than a discount store. It's better therapy than any shrink (no matter how much you buy, it's still cheaper in the long run); it's better than yoga (take it from us, pawing through the racks *is* relaxing) and going every day is a better fix than any drug. Don't mind the communal dressing rooms — nobody is looking at you, they're looking to see if what you're trying on is better than what they're trying on. You know you're hooked when you know the code for every designer brand they carry. We can't reveal them here, but for the uninitiated (are there any left?) here is a guide to deciphering a Loehmann's label.

Size — Everything cute is usually a size 4 or 6, so it's worth it to diet-yourself-to-death.

Designer Code — We'll tell you this one, WV is Finity and, if you spot an EIS, grab it, it's Perry Ellis at a fraction of the retail price.

Fabric Content — No polyester, no matter how much of a bargain it may seem.

Price — Keep an eye out for double mark-downs, you can get an Anne Klein suit for about 1/4 of what you'd pay retail. If the season's almost over, save it for next, at these prices, it's worth it.

Garment Classification — Jacket, coats, blouses, accessories, read the label. You may not be able to tell just from looking what the article of clothing is, that's why it's so inexpensive.

Not so long ago and not quite far away there lived a very happy Princess. There were stars in her eyes, a smile on her face, and a rock on the third finger of her left hand.

She no longer considered the faraway lands as the place from whence her Prince would come, but rather as the place to which he would take her on their honeymoon.

The entire kingdom of Suburbia was rejoicing on this the Princess' Wedding Day. 300 guests had gathered to watch the Princess float down the aisle on her father's arm, accompanied by 12 bridesmaids, 14 ushers, a flower girl and assorted grandparents.

Waiting under the Chuppa was her curly-haired prince, promising to love, honor and keep her in the style to which she was accustomed.

Onward then . . . to the Main Event

THE PRINCESS' WEDDING

Good-by Columbus

GOODBYE COLUMBUS

From birth, the Princess hears "the happiest day of my life will be the day I dance at your wedding!"

Now that THE DAY is here the Princess can understand why it's such a big *magillah*. Between her mother and Vivian the bridal consultant, not one detail has been left unattended to. It's an extravaganza that uses every trick in the book.

Traditional brides opt for a temple wedding, even though it means no picture taking during the ceremony. The contemporary Princess demands no less than the ballroom of the city's finest hotel. Whichever she chooses, the Princess, et. al., will pull out all the stops to insure that hers is a wedding by which all others pale in comparison.

This is where the wedding consultant entrs the picture. Usually a frustrated career bride, this harried woman runs herself ragged, selecting commemorative stamps for the invitations that will coordinate with the centerpieces. And on the night of the wedding she is invaluable in keeping the schnorers from wrapping up the sweet table pastries even before the wedding cake is cut. And, of course, her presence is also necessary for keeping the peace between the Princess and her mother.

This moment is by far the happiest in the princess' life, to be rivaled only by the day she will dance at HER daughter's wedding.

CULTIVATING CARATS

Or . . . Selecting a Stone Suitable for Upgrading

Most Princesses will agree that you start with a carat and work your way up! A stone this size requires a cleverly designed setting to make it look larger than it really is. If someone remarks on the size, the Princess just replies that it's a flawless stone, implying that it will be upgraded sometime in the near future.

SIZE GUIDE

To determine just how much of a gem your fiance really is — simply place your stone on the handy reference guide below.

You must be marrying for love	SMALL	♦
You take this guy for love or money	MEDIUM	◆
It's as easy to love a rich man as a poor one.	LARGE	◆

Overheard in Marshall Field's Bridal Registry:

Princess #1: Did you see Rhoda's ring, it's four karats?

Princess #2: Really? What shape is it, isn't it a little ostentatious?

Princess #1: Pear and no, she just lists to the left now.

Princess #2: Do you think the stone was in his family?

Princess #1: No, the only stones in his family are the rocks in his head!

Meeting the Machetenum

No matter how long you've been engaged, nothing has prepared you or your parents for the meeting of the machatootsies. This is best done on neutral territory (in the Princess' parent's home) so everyone can begin making plans for the wedding.

The smartest strategy is to have the parents-in-law meet before the Prince and Princess arrive on the scene. That way they can establish their own craziness.

Your arrival only adds to the confusion. Even if the in-laws get along famously the Princess and her mother can still find plenty to argue about. Soon everybody will be choosing up sides and the Royal battle will begin, for better or worse. Everything from the guest list to the menu is a potential source for conflagration.

WHAT THEY SAY	WHAT THEY MEAN
Mother of Bride:	
Just give us your list and let us know how many you want to invite.	I'm paying for this wedding and they're not getting more than 50 guests.
Mother of Groom:	
You've done a wonderful job... your daughter really knows what she wants.	I can't believe I have to put up with *both* of them now!
Father of the Bride:	
So, tell me again, how many years has your son been in college?	No daughter of mine is going to starve. I'll take him into the business if I have to.
Father of the Groom:	
Sam, you're so lucky to have such a lovely daughter. I only have sons.	Thank God! *He'll* be bankrupt after this affair, not me.

Q. How do you stop a Princess from being a nympho-maniac?

A. Marry her.

Jewish Star Wars

1) BATTLE OF THE GUEST LIST

The number of guests to be invited to the wedding changes from hour to hour. Inviting Cousin Freida and her entourage of 12 means reducing the groom's list by another baker's dozen. After all, who's paying for this affair. Also, the bride and groom must constantly remind their parents that this *is their* wedding, and couldn't they invite at least a friend or two.

2) THE INVITATION SKIRMISH

The wording of the invitation is as controversial as that of the Camp David Accords. Do the bride's parents **cordially invite you** or **request the honor of your presence?** And what about the groom? Is his title used as a tip-off off as to what a catch he is?

And do his parents make the credits, too?

2) DRESS WARS

Is black tie a must or not even considered as as option? Will the mothers wear short or long? The Princess will always wear a white gown, no matter how colored her past, and pastels are for mints with her initials, never for the usher's tuxes, and the brides-maids are pretty as posies in dresses that always match the blooms in the centerpieces.

4) THE FOOD FEUD

Fish, foul or filet, it must be kosher if the Rabbi's going to stay. The key here is to over order. Never let it be said that anyone didn't go home stuffed from YOUR wedding.

If the machetenum cannot agree on anything else, they will at least *always* agree that the Princess and their Prince are a match made in heaven.

THE LADIES
IN WAITING

Or . . . Always a Bridesmaid

Even though every one of the Princess's friends complains about being a bridesmaid, *God Forbid you shouldn't ask her.* So it's perfectly acceptable for the Princess to have ten Jewish lovelies proceed her down the aisle. Especially since she's proceeding them to the chuppa. Candidates for this honor are chosen from the ranks of childhood friends, college roommates, sorority sisters, cousins, and don't forget future sisters-in-law. A CAUTIONARY NOTE: No children in the processional, particularly darling little PITs who might steal the show.

It's best, if possible, to select bridesmaids with similar body types. Finding a dress that all ten girls can agree upon is hard enough without adding the headache of trying to squeeze one zaftig Princess into an off the shoulder size 14 that can only be worn with a strapless bra. ANOTHER CAUTIONARY NOTE: it may be a good idea to find a gown that no one likes so everyone can be equally unhappy.

SPECIAL HONORS ACCORDED TO THE BRIDESMAIDS.

1) Priviledge of spending too much on a faux taffeta dress only to be worn for this one occasion. Be prepared to spend in excess of $100 (not including alterations, yet.)

And then there are the accoutrements . . . dyed to match shoes, so uncomfortable they'll never make it to the *hora* . . . special strapless bra for that backless gown . . . long slip (if you're lucky you may have one left from the last wedding) . . . trip to the beauty shop. If your hair looks great, maybe no one will notice that you look like a clone from the neck down.

2) Privilege of giving a bride a shower. Once the bride and bridesmaids are on speaking terms again after selecting those hideous dresses, the bridesmaids must entertain for the Princess. If all the girls are lucky enough to have boyfriends, it's acceptable to make a couples party in the evening. But, if even one of the group is solo, it means a shower in the afternoon. The only male in attendance should be the Princess' fiance, who presents the Princess with a "surprise" gift that the Princess should always pick out herself to avoid any embarrassment.

SHOWER THEMES

1. Around-the-clock shower
2. Recipe shower
3. Kitchen shower
4. Bar/Entertainment Shower
5. Sexual Device shower (of course this entails bringing a gag gift. In other words, the princess gags at the thought of using it)
6. Personal shower
7. Fun and Games shower
8. Gadget shower
9. Wine and cheese shower
10. Miscellaneous shower

No matter what the theme, it is essential to bring a poem to each pre-nuptial affair.

bloome
CHICAGO

DRESS REHEARSAL

The Princess has been practicing her part for years at her bat mitzvah and sweet 16 and now, before the chuppa goes up, there is *erev* of wedding. Everyone in the wedding party gathers to go through a dry run of the ceremony, and this prenuptial practice always brings on a few pre-nuptial tears from the princess' mother and soon to be mother-in-law, while the ushers make cracks about always a bridesmaid, finally a bride. No one ever gets their part straight but they go on to a lavish dinner anyway. The groom's mother is always sad, knowing this is the last meal she'll ever be able to feed him while he's still her little boy. And the bride's mother is distraught, not because she's losing her daughter, but because they've served chicken at this meal, too. (Is there still time to change the menu for the wedding?) After much tasting and toasting, everyone goes home to get a good night's sleep. (Except the princess that is, who nervously polishes off the pint of Hagen Dazs in her mother's freezer.)

Mr. and Mrs. Abe B. Schneider

request the honour of your presence

at the marriage of their daughter

Sharon Paula

to

Mr. Glenn Steven Liss

son of Mr. and Mrs. Albert Liss

on Sunday, the third of August

Nineteen hundred and sixty-nine

at six o'clock

The Ambassador West Hotel

Chicago, Illinois

Black Tie

The Princess' Wedding

THE MAIN EVENT

The night of nights has finally arrived, the one for which the Princess was born. The night begins at dawn and goes something like this . . .

8:00 a.m. — Princess awakens feeling guilty about eating the Hagen Dazs. What if her wedding gown doesn't fit?

9:00 a.m. — Princess goes to the beauty shop with her mother and her veil . . . (Princess fights with her mother. Princess: "Why couldn't the beauty operator have come to the house? I can't believe I have to walk around with this veil on my head all day." Mother: "See, mother always knows best. Aren't you glad I talked you out of cathedral length."

10:00 a.m. — After having her recombed 6 times, it's time for the Princess' manicure. Only pale pink will do. Coral may look dated in the wedding album five years from now. Allow an extra half hour for nail wrapping. God forbid a broken nail should spoil the whole evening.

11:00 a.m. — Return home and get your gown ready to go.

12:00 NOON — Go immediately to a suite at the hotel where the makeup artist begins the transformation.

1:00 p.m. — Order up lunch. Too nervous to eat. Can only manage three orders of french fries and a sip of Tab.

2:30 p.m. — Sit around for several hours with bridesmaids reminiscing about old boyfriends and how you finally found yuor Prince . . . and how they should get so lucky. Tactful bridesmaids will refrain from telling the Princess how charming her Prince was to them the night before.

3:00 p.m. — Nothing else to do. Fight with your mother.

4:00 p.m. — Run out of things to fight with your mother about. Start to lament about your future mother-in-law. Finally you may have a new opponent.

5:00 p.m. — Everyone is finally dressed. Spend the next

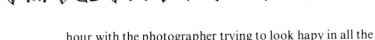

hour with the photographer trying to look hapy in all the pictures. All the while worrying about your hair.

5:30 p.m. — The guests begin to arrive to strains of chamber music for a 6:00 ceremony. Start wondering if it's too late to back out now, and get angry at the groom because you're wondering if he's thinking the same thing.

6:30 p.m. — Ceremony begins only 1/2 hour late. There's no turning back now. Stand poised at the beginning of the aisle while the cantor sings "Because" with a yiddish accent, and realize that you've finally made it.

6:32 p.m. — Float down the aisle thrilling to the sounds of gasps and a hint of the phrase . . . "OH MY isn't she a gorgeous bride."

6:34 p.m. — Arrive at chuppa.

6:42 p.m. — Guests laugh as groom guzzles much more than his share of the wine.

6:54 p.m. — Groom breaks glass. Guests yell "Mazel Tov" . . . you breathe a sigh of relief. The recessional begins to the music of the bride's favorite . . . Barry Manilow's, "It's a Miracle!"

7:00 p.m. — Stand in mile long line receiving best wishes, wet kisses and fat envelopes.

7:30 p.m. — Reception with butler service begins. White gloved waiters pass trays bearing miniature egg rolls, knishes, quiche, stuffed mushrooms, smoked salmon (lox) pate (chopped liver), chicken wings, mini-meatballs, hotdogs wrapped in dough (called this bvecause pigs in the blanket certainly don't sound kosher), crudites with dip, mounds of cold shrimp, and, of course, the mandatory Champagne.

8:30 p.m. — Guests move to the ballroom for dinner and

dancing. Last minute anxi_y strikes over seating arrangements. Aunt Fanny en_d up at the same table with cousin Ilene.

8:30 p.m. — The band leader _ounces — MR. AND MRS. SHELDON RIGHT . . . _l stand and applaud the Princess' accomplishment.

8:35 p.m. — The flaming fruit appetizers appear.

8:45 p.m. — Salad with choice of dressing comes next. Fight with mother . . . you wanted Caesars.

8:55 p.m. — The Consomme. Your grandmother wants to know *"So nu?* What would have been wrong with throwing in a little *Knaidlach?"*

9:10 p.m. — Waiters wheel out silver salvers and begin to carve the prime rib. Also begin pouring the white wine. (No one would have accepted red unless it was Manaschewitz.)

9:12 p.m. — Fight with your mother about the glazed carrots. She says, "Fight with your husband, you're his problem now."

9:15 p.m. — It's time for the first dance as Mr. and Mrs. Bride and Groom take center stage to the strains of "Endless Love." Feeling left out, your father cuts in and your HUSBAND asks your mother to dance while the groom's mother sits out the first dance, sulking.

9:30 p.m. — Everyone joins the happy family and the fun really begins in earnest as the bandleader strikes up *havanagillah* and the *segues* into the hora. Ten ushers all lift the b ride and groom on chairs. (Thank God the Princess dieted.)

11:00 p.m. — Out come the sweets to revive the revellers.

11:02 p.m. — The wedding cake is ceremoniously rolled out on a gilt serving cart and all the guests crowd around to get a glimpse as the Princess and her Prince take the first bite. The Prince digs in while the Princess picks delicately. She plans to gain her 10 pounds in the first *year* not the first hour of her marriage.

11:15 p.m. — Continental coffee service with brandy and Cognac follows.

12:00 — Bridge and groom are anxious for the last guests to leave so they can tally the take. Mother's glad she doesn't have to watch the maid clean up after *this* party.

Sweet Table Strategies

No matter how lovely the bridal party looks, how gorgeous the chuppa, how delicious the dinner . . . nothing is as important as setting the sweets on a table so laden it may collapse. Why you ask? Because these goodies are the only thing the guest can take home.

Never worry about everyone getting their fill at the wedding. Strategic moves for cutting a swath through the sweet table include taking two plates and a friend. What one of you might miss, the other will find.

In order to get everything on your plate at once it often becomes necessary to cut a sliver of this and a morsel of that. After having tasted everything, you can then return for seconds of your favorites and even some for the road. (Note: this is the only time of the evening when it is appropriate to serve paper napkins for carryouts)

Princess' Floral Dilemma

"I got married on February 17th because it was the only date the band had free for the next six months. But this created another problem: it was impossible to get enough roses because all had been used for Valentine's Day. Even Ronsley could not beg, borrow or steal enough of these special buds to cover the chuppa, the bables and the bridesmaids. I needn't have owrried though. Fortunately, they created a gorgeous setting with hot house lilies and orchids surrounding an authentic pond which could only be reached by crossing a tiny bridge (my mother always loved Monet) and the ladies at the club were buzzing for months.

Arlene Farber Golden
Miami

Whether it be a Viennese Table in NYC or an Ultra Chocolate Bar in Columbus, these mega-categories add up to a glorious finale to any Princess' wedding:

Watermelon basket with melon balls
Flourless Chocolate cake with creme fraiche
Fraise de bois with creme fraiche
Chocolate dipped marshmellows and strawberries
Strawberry and Chocolate Chip Cheese cake
Slalvah
Frozen white chocolate mousse in chocolate cups
White chocolate coated pretzels
Wedding Cake
Napolean
Sacher Tortes
Petit Fours
Kiwi Tarts
Chocolate Pecan Pie
Eclairs
Kermits
Marzipan
Chocolate dipped fruit
Taffy apple tree
Black Forest Cake
Croque et Boche
Cherries Jubilee
Crepe Suzette
Pastel Mints
Strudel
Homantashen
Kolachkes
Bakalava
Fresh fruit
Butter cookies
Peche melba
Flan
Poires belles helene
Baked Alaska
Floating islands
Chocolate truffles

FORBIDDEN FRUITS

Singing Sabra relatives performing Israeli folktunes.

Serving Dinner family style

Guests wearing polyester

Keeping the bar open during dinner (wine or champagne should be served by white gloved waiters throughout the meal).

Finger sandwiches (or anything with mayonnaise) served as hor d'oeuvres.

Not having a live band. (This is not a Bar Mitzvah and a D.J. won't do.)

Fresh flowers only. (This is the only time dried silk flowers are gauche.)

TALLYING THE TAKE

Although the bridal suite is breathtaking, the newlyweds are oblivious to its beauty. More seductive than the bulge in the groom's trousers is the bulge of envelopes in his jacket pocket. Lest you think the Princess is a calculating bride, she must add up the contents of these envelopes by hand. Endorsing the checks with her new last name is an orgasmic way for the Princess to begin her honeymoon.

All of this monetary foreplay leaves the couple spent but still the Princess changes into one of the myriad of matching peignoir sets and a romantic evening ensues.

Forbidden Fruits

1. Call mother

2. Break out the brewskys and watch X-rated movies on the closed circuit T.V.

3. Have a headache

4. Wear a Lanz nightgown

5. Call mother

6. Order hotdogs and beans from room service

7. Have a headache

8. Write thank you notes

9. Call mother

10. Let him party with ushers while you gossip with bridesmaids

11. Wash your hair and put it in a "going to sleep hairdo"

12. Think of names for the children

13. Have a fight

14. Have a headache

15. Call your mother.

The Endless Search for Non-Humid Honeymoon Spots

You know the line: "'till death do us part." Well, that just might not be too far off because you'd just *die* if your hair frizzed on your honeymoon. It's not so bad after you have a suntan, when masses of curls might look exotic but if your hair looks like it could get on the sight-seeing bus on its own, before you've even collected the luggage . . . you're in trouble.

Unfortunately, all the most romantic places are too humid for the average Princess but, to help you out, we've studied all the spots and the ten below will give you at least a fighting chance.

1. Arizona — Although no one feels like spending their honeymoon in a retirement community, your hair will look great while you're doing nothing.

2. Acapulco — Although it's humid, you can use your blow dryer and hot rollers at all the big hotels. It's foreign but not frizzy.

3. Hawaii — Moderately humid but you can put beautiful flowers behind your ear and the romance will save your honeymoon from ruin.

4. Greek Islands — A cruise here is fabulous but avoid July and August.

5. Italy — Especially in Florence and Milan the shopping is so great you don't have time to be upset about your hair.

6. California — Varied climate and you can drive up Highway 1 enjoying the sights from an air conditioned rent-a-car.

7. Rio de Janeiro — If you caught a guy who will take you here, who cares about anything else.

8. Colorado — Skiing for a winter wedding. Great because you can sit in the lodge looking perfectly coiffed wearing chic ski clothes without any danger of breaking a leg.

9. Israel — Not only is it a great honeymoon, it's a mitzvah as well. And there's not a drop of moisture in the Negev.

10. The Islands — Aruba, Bermuda, St. Maarten, St. Croix, St. Barts, St. Kitts, St. Thomas, Paradise Island, Eleutheria, Martinique, Guadeloupe, Barbados. Don't bother bringing your blow dryer. You won't miss it in the idyllic paradise spots. Go Native!

Standing in the bedroom of her Palace, the Queen gazed into her mirror and asked, "Mirror, mirror on the wall, who's the JAPiest of them all?" Of course, she didn't expect an answer but she smiled at her reflection as she counted her blessings: Her husband Stan, a successful dentist; a modern, split level in the right suburb with her own tennis courts and five carats divided into a pair of earrings and an upgraded engagement ring and a little P.I.T. who was already following in her footsteps.

But soon her smile was replaced by a frown as the Queen, nee Princess noticed lines at the corner of her eyes. Was 34 too early for an eye job? Perhaps a week at La Costa would help and losing five pounds wouldn't hurt either. Maybe her best friend Helene would go, they could leave their kids with their mother . . . and Stan could fend for himself for a few days.

CHAPTER 7

The Promised Land

PRINCESS AS QUEEN

Sadie, Sadie,
Married Lady

Sadie, Sadie, Married Lady

Now that the Princess no longer feels compelled to impress *her* business associates, her energy is directed at impressing her husband's colleagues instead. Depending on her spouse's profession there are certain rules of etiquette which must be followed:

The Mercantile Wife:
Instead of a downpayment on a house, this bridegroom is gifted with a seat on the commodities exchange. Because trading for the day is over between 2 and 4 o'clock, the Princess' social life revolves around afternoons at a posh health club, moving on to coke and cocktails and an early dinner because the market opens early in the morning. The smart Mercantile Princess knows not only the value of a dollar, but the value of a yen, mark, and t-bill and is conversant in the strategies of amassing gold, ginny maes and eurodollars, as well. Mercantile wives sport perpetual tans, gold Rolexes and multi-karat diamonds. Extravagent but casual entertaining is her forte.

Mrs. M.D.
The sacrifices she made to put her husband through medical or dental school absolve this Princess of any guilt she might have for spending the doctor's money as fast as he makes it. She matches her husband's selfless career with philanthropic pursuits of her own. She serves on the women's auxiliary of his

hospital and chairs the yearly tennis party for her chapter of the Heart Association. She is responsible for organizing their social life and making sure her husband's tux is pressed for the annual A.M.A. dinnerdance.

The Legal Partner
Though she dreamed of being a June bride, this Princess waited until August. The aggrevation of frizzy hair wouldn't come close to the aggrevation she'd have if the wedding was held before her husband-to-be sat for the bar. Now that they're legal, she has ample opportunity to use her formal china and silver entertaining the senior partners in her husband's firm. This is particularly true if the senior partner is married to the Princess' mother-in-law.

Their annual vacation is spent in the same spot where the American Bar Assoc. Convention is held. This year it's in San Francisco. Because it's a write-off, the Princess has no trouble talking her husband into letting her spend more on resort-wear.

CPA Spouse
There's no accounting for taste, especially when the months from January through April are so taxing for this Princess. She spends these months planning a no-holes-barred vacation beginning April 16th to make up for 5 months of solo social engagements. Staid though CPA's might be, what goes on in the off-season is nobody's business.

The Care and Feeding of a Queen

No matter what professional idiosyncrasies Mrs. Princess must endure, there is one thing these women have in common: their husbands all treat them like Queens. Now that the honeymoon is over they have become adept at giving the Princess what she thinks she wants, but they both know she doesn't need:

1. Flagstone patio
2. Daily maid
3. Expensive, sporty second car
4. Hot tub
5. Swimming pool
6. Tennis court
7. Yacht
8. Seats at $100 bond dinner
9. Box seat season football tickets (clever Prince)
10. Betamax and wide screen TV

Recipe for a Jewish Heartburn

Kreplach
Kneidlach (matzo balls)
Schmaltz herring
Mandlach
Flanken in the pot
Kasha varnishkes
Lathke
Kishke
Cabbage or beet borscht
Gefilte fish with horse-
    radish
Matzo brei
Lucshon kugel
Gedempte
Knishes
Pastrami, corned beef,
    chopped liver

Quiz —
The Slipper's
on the Other Foot

The Princess has reached that point in time when she is the guiltor instead of the guiltee. She has miraculously forgotten her vow to "never do that to *my* children." Take this quiz to determine how much guilt is really enough.

---

1. Although you've never been enamoured of your mother-in-law, you've been driving her to her mah jong game with her ladyfriends for the past 18 years. Now that your daughter is old enough to drive isn't it fair to have her take over this task?

YES — It's the least she could do. Grandma's old and she may not get this chance much longer.

NO — Suffer, but not in silence, it's good leverage ' with your husband.

---

2. Your daughter, who is in college 400 miles away, asks if she can spend her winter vacation with her boyfriend's family at their Miami Beach condo. You answer:

YES — Go ahead, who cares if it's a shonda for the neighbors to go half-way around the country when you haven't seen your father for 3 months.

NO — But why don't you invite him to come here, he can sleep in your brother's room.

---

3. You're planning your daughter's wedding and already have the 200+ guest list drawn up when your daughter springs the bad news. She wants a small ceremony in the rabbi's study, after all, she's 32. You say:

YES — Go ahead, deprive your mother of the one thing she's lived for all her life.

NO — Does she want everyone to think what they thought about Mrs. Bromberg's daughter who eloped last year.

Q. What is the difference between a vulture and a Jewish wife?

A. The vulture waits until you're dead to eat your heart out.

Chic in Suburbia

After a two year tour of duty in the city the Princess and her husband are ready to move to the suburbs. In suburbia the Princess need only worry about "Keeping up with the Jacobs" and not about getting mugged on the way home from the office. She can have a spacious lawn and patio with Brown Jordan outdoor furniture that doesn't have to be shlepped inside every night. She'll choose a neighborhood with good schools and a good temple . . . and a good shopping mall with plenty of parking.

As you might have guessed, the impetus for this major move is the decision for the Princess to start having little JAPlets of her own. Why this decision? Not only is it the next logical step but everybody else is doing it and what self respecting Princess would allow her little darlings to grow up without all the luxuries *she* had as a child?

Once she has her children she must have a place to put them. From breakfast nook to nursery, the Princess' Palace will be a reflection of herself. Her new suburban taste favors track lighting and Italian furniture molded from plastic, not covered with it. All the gilt edged avocado green and gold memories of her childhood are banished from her home which is decorated in the most up-to-date style. And, when mother comes to visit, the Princess receives kudos and compliments: "It's lovely dear, of course, it's not *my* taste but if that's what they're showing . . .I'm going to get you some dried silk flowers for that Kosta Boda vase."

Instead of dealing with crowds on busses or fighting for cabs the Princess is now arranging car pools and tennis schedules. Her mornings are free for having her nails wrapped and whittling down her waist at exercise class. Her afternoons are spent lunching with the girls from La Maze class and by then it's time to make reservations for dinner. The Princess has arrived. But what's next? A condo in Florida? A house in the Hamptons? The possibilities are endless for the Princess as Queen.

6 Spots for a Summer Condo

1. Hamptons, N.Y.
2. Catskills, N.Y.
3. South Haven, MI.
4. Nippersink, WI.
5. Long Boat Key, FL.
6. Palm Springs, CA.

THE VIRTUES OF VOLUNTEERING
ORT as a sport

The Princess is always willing to donate her time and money to help those less fortunate than she in the name of her homeland. Israeli Bonds, planting trees, reclamation of the desert, desalination of the Dead Sea . . . are all worthy causes. While she puts her pennies in each of their pushkes, she generally puts her time into only one of them.

Choosing between B'nai Brith, ORT, Pioneer Woman, and Hadassah isn't easy. It's best to go to a meeting of each to determine which group of women you can best befriend and impress. Once you've made your decision it's time to roll up your Perry Ellis sleeves (allowing ample display of your gold and diamonds. Make sure you choose a group of women who go to the right hairdresser and who meet at a location convenient to the place you get your nails wrapped.

Lox Boxes:
Appeal not only to the pocket, but to the palate as well. Preparations begin months in advance when women approach local merchants for donations of food and little tsatkes. The real troupers in this endeavor are the volunteers' husbands who get up at 6:00 am to deliver the boxes. This repast includes ½ pound of lox, a dozen bagels, Philadelphia cream cheese, danish, orange juice, key chains and plastic rain bonnets.

Rummage Sales:
Held in the social hall of the temple on Sunday afternoon. The idea is to sell the contents of your crawlspace and basement to raise enough money to add a new wing to the temple. At the end of the day, most of the stuff has to be donated to the Misrachi resale shop because who in their right mind would buy anyone elses old schmates?

Walk for Israel:
Route is 18 miles long for Chi and checkpoints are located at Jewish Community Centers and delicatessens. Pre-teen walkers solicit per-mile-pledges and their mothers donate one dollar per mile to aussage their guilt for not walking themselves.

Fashion Shows:
Hard to distinguish the models from the matrons — they're all dressed alike. Menu features chicken salad in pineapple boats. The ladies have 1 glass of white wine and go home with a headache. These affairs always cost their husbands more than the donation because someone will invariably suggest they go to Saks for some shopping after the show.

QUEEN'S CLOSET

6 pairs wool gab pants

42 sweaters (in sweater bags)

26 silk blouses (all in cleaner's bags)

10 cotton blouses (not broadcloth)

31 T-shirts

18 tennis outfits

12 pairs of shorts

8 pairs designer jeans (varying length)

13 blazers (many still with tags)

4 Nipon cocktail dresses

15 silk dresses (some for work, some for play)

16 skirts (assorted styles)

7 bathrobes (terry galore, long and short)

27 belts

68 pairs of shoes (including boots)

40 purses

17 bathing suits (one piece & two)

11 jogging outfits

Annex (The Front Closet)

6 wool coats
2 leather jackets
4 cotton jackets
3 furs (1 coat — 2 jackets)
1 trendy trench
2 down coats

ORT Taste and Tell:

Held before Passover, this is an event where all the young Jewish matrons add matzoh meal to their favorite yontif recipe and bring it to share with their ORT group. After teasing the other members with a little taste, each reveals the secret ingredients and calorie count of the dish. Then they Xerox the recipes into a binder and use them as a successful fundraiser.

GUIDE TO THE SUBURBS

Suburban Princesses are concentrated in the suburbs shown on this map. Of course, you'll find them in other spots, especially where the major merchants have started opening branches.

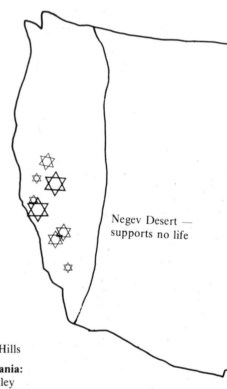

Negev Desert — supports no life

Illinois:
Skokie
Highland Park
Wilmette
Deerfield
Northbrook
Buffalo Grove
Flossmoor
Lincolnwood
West Rogers Park
Budlong Woods

Florida:
Miami Beach
North Miami Beach
Kendall
Hallendale
Emerald Hills
Plantation
Hollywood
West Palm Beach
Pompano Beach
Boca Raton
Coconut Grove
Coral Gables
Tamarac
Inverrary
Coral Springs
Jacaranda
Pembroke Pines
Deerfield Beach

Washington, D.C.
Falls Church
Alexandria
Chevy Chase
Silver Spring
Potomac
Pikesville

Kansas:
Mission Hills

Pennsylvania:
Penn Valley
Squirrel Hill

Missouri:
Clayton
Chesterfield
Creve Coeur
La Due

Ohio:
Upper Arlington
Bexley
Eastmoor
Shaker Heights
Amberly Village

New Jersey:
Fort Lee
Cherry Hill

Massachusetts:
Brookline
Newton
West Newton
Brighton

Texas:
Fondren South West
Memorial
Highland Park

New York:
Great Neck
Roslyn
Manhasset Hills
Westbury
Jericho
Cedarhurst
Hewlett
Woodmere
Oceanside
Valley Stream
Scarsdale
New Rochelle
Syracuse
Forest Hills

California:
Westwood
Beverly Hills
Marina Del Rey
Hollywood
Santa Monica
Culver City
Brentwood
Encino Valley

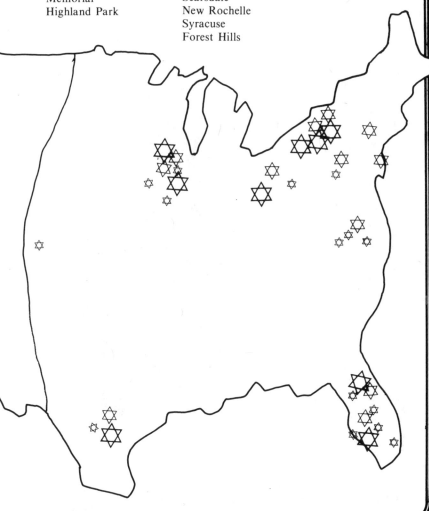

WHAT? . . . I SHOULD CLEAN?
Help in the House

The word "chores" is not in the Princess' vocabulary. For this reason she must hire someone to do them for her. The going rate for this once-a-week help is $35.00 per day and carfare.

The Princess considers this money well spent. Her floors are clean enough to eat off of; her moldings are so dust-free they could pass the white glove test; her beds are so well made a dime will bounce off the sheets. All this and her manicure remains flawless.

Rumor has it that, "just to make sure", the Princess follows the cleaning lady around the house with a dust rag. Maybe this is why she is always exhausted at the end of the maid's day and must be taken out to dinner.

Q. How many Princesses does it take to change a lightbulb?

A. Two. One to call daddy and one to pour the TAB.

DIAL-A-GUILT-TRIP #3

Princess: Hello?

Mother: Hi dear.

Princess: Oh, mother, it's you.

Mother: Who should it be? Is your son feeling OK?

Princess: What do you mean, "my son." Don't you call him David anymore?

Mother: He was playing outside. He could have caught a draft.

Princess: Mother . . . it's July and you had him dressed in two sweaters, his baseball cap and a jacket.

Mother: It's been so long since I've seen him I forgot his name already. But last week when he slept over he was hot and wringing wet.

Princess: A draft? You don't even turn your air-conditioning on when it's 90 degrees!

Mother: So what are you and Arthur doing this weekend?

Princess: Why?

Mother: Your father wants you to come for dinner but he'll understand if you're too busy.

Princess: Well, now that you mention it . . . David did say he wanted to see his grandpa so maybe we could drop him off on our way the club.

Mother: And what about you and Arthur? You can't make time? You leave your son like a gypsy . . . wait until he grows up and you never see him!

Princess: OK mother, but don't make chaleh, I'm on Scarsdale.

JAPmobiles

Princesses don't walk, they drive. To carpool, to the store, to the beauty shop, to the cleaners, to the mailbox. Obviously their car is very important . . . it's one third of their life! Not just any car will do. The Princess' car is chosen to compliment her jewels and furs . . . mileage be damned!

Porsche 911, 928
Mercedes 450-SL

Bought under the guise of indulging her husband, these models help the Princess regain her lost youth while forcing her insurance to skyrocket (Automatic transmission only . . . Princesses do not drive stick!)

Cadillacs (all models
except Cimmaron)

Truly a status symbol in silver or powder blue. Only option not available is a Cuisenart. Good for transporting grandparents. Get a sunroof so, when it's your car pool day, you'll be sure to sit in the sun.

Saab Turbo
BMW 320i
Datsun 280-ZX

These are good "starter cars" for the Prince who hasn't made it yet. Expensive enough to let you know he's still got a good chance of going somewhere.

Pick-ups
Vans
Jeeps

Only forbidden fruits drive these. Better to go to exercise class than go on a date with someone who drives something like this.

Car Cosmetics

Colors: Light blue, silver, bronze, brown, yellow, red, white, grey. Any new-for-198- shade is always the first color choice.

Upholstery: Velour, leather. Never vinyl.

Windows: Tinted glass, always electric (Princesses don't do windows).

Dashboard: LED for all instrumentation. Contents of glove compartment: Kleenex, rain bonnet, Wash n' Dries.

Vanity plates: Name or euphemism for your husband's profession.

One dark night as Muffy Hughes Fairchild strolled the cobbled avenues of the upper east side, a sense of fear and foreboding came upon her. For, in the distance there arose an unearthly glow. Closer and closer the light came and she began to shake in her Topsiders. Could this be a close encounter?

As the humanoid approached, Muffy realized the glow was emminated from the profusion of gold and diamond jewelry which bedecked the female apparition. Was she from another planet? As far as Muffy was concerned she might well have been . . . she was from Long Island. The creature extended her manicured hand in a gesture of friendship and began to speak:

Princess: I've been shlepping all night. This neb I was out with wanted to pick up a six-pack and go to a polo match.

Muffy: Neb? Schlepp? I don't understand!

Princess: I thought I'd plotz, his car was full of chazerei.

Muffy: Plotz? Chazerei? If only I could communicate with her?

Well Muffy can and so can you . . .

A DICTIONARY
OF JEWISH
JARGON

*You Don't Have
to be Jewish*

Jewish Jargon

A a

Allowance: Often confused by the Princess with Federal Reserve Funds.

Ancestors: Early generations of Princess' relatives who came to this country by boat (which was *not* named the Mayflower).

Chazerei: Derived from the work chazei, someone who can never get enough. Unnecessary excesses with which the Princess surrounds herself.

Chuppa: Marriage canopy. More decorative than symbolic.

Credit Cards: 2" x 3" rectangular pieces of plastic (containing the name of her father or husband) used by the Princess as the keys to her Kingdom.

Diet: Way of life for the Princess. Even the best ones are made to be broken.

Erev: Refers to the night on which candles are lit and the Jewish holidays begin. Similar in concept to New Year's Eve.

Fleischech: Never mix with milchech. Separate utensils are required for these meat based dishes.

Forbidden fruit: 1. Anything that causes guilt. 2. Anything the Princess would not be caught dead wearing, doing or dating.

Gold: 14k or 18k, the armour a Princess wears.

Guilt: Jewish heredity disease. Symptoms include a churning stomach and feelings of deep-seated anxiety. Highly contagious, expecially when the Princess spends too much time in the company of her mother.

H h

Haagen Daz: Now that it's available West of the Hudson, Princesses everywhere are gaining megapounds vie Chocolate-Chocolate Chip, with hot fudge, no less. (Note to Prince: Promise her anything but give her Haagen-Daz)

Hadassah Baroque: Decorating style favored by the mothers of Princesses. Hallmark is copious amounts of gilt and velour.

Haftorah: The portion of the five books of Moses that is the Princess' Bat Mitzvah script.

Kinder: The group of junior JAPs who haven't yet made it into the dining room for the holidays.

Kvetch: Princess' approach to getting her own way. Tactics include whining, grumbling, moaning, crying and other non-stop complaining.

M m

M&Ms: Bits of chocolate coated candy. They are never around long enough to melt in the Princess' hand. Always served at parties and often the only items in the Princess' otherwise empty refrigerator.

Machetenum: Two opposing camps of parents who pretend to

Miami Beach: Often confused with the promised land because it promises a great tan and a chance to be seen by all the other MOTs.

Milchich: Dairy products according to the Kosher dietary laws. Includes blintzes, lox, cream cheese & bagels, kugel & knishes all of which play a prominent role in breaking the Yom Kippur fast. (Note: Ratner's Kosher Deli on New York's lower East side is a mecca to Miechich). Also see fleichech.

get along because their kinderlach are getting married.

Meiskiet: Princess before her nose job, braces and hair straightening.

Mishpocha: The Jewish holiday group. Includes cousins once or twice removed.

Money: The ultimate aphrodisiac. (Credit cards also acceptable)

M.O.T.: Member of the Tribe. A player in the game of Jewish geography.

Mother: See guilt.

Mrs.: Most sought after degree at college. Favorite post-graduate study as well.

Nebbish: (Neb), Fix-up date your mother would think is cute.

Network: Modern day replacement for the matchmaker. Provides a valuable service, that of finding suitable dates (mates) for Princesses everywhere.

N.J.B.: Nice Jewish Boy. Perfect potential Prince. A date the Princess would think was cute.

P p

P.I.T.: Princess-in-Training, junior JAP.

Plotz: Drop dead (Not actually, just for effect).

Polyester: What?

Princess: See pages 1 thru 144.

Retail: Form of commerce to which the Princess has a great aversion and in which she will only engage if no one can get it for her wholesale.

S s

Sammy: Curly haired brothers of the Sigma Alpha Mu fraternity. Demographics of Alumnus are: high income, home owning and married.

Schmutz: *Never* found in a Princess home. Literally: dirt.

Shagits: Blond haired, blue eyed forbidden fruit who ends up marrying a shiksa.

Shtetle: Small village in the old country. Origin of Princess' ancestors and the fiddler on the roof.

Shiksa: Blond haired, blue eyed competition for the Princess. Any girl who is not a MOT.

Schlepp: Refers to the carrying around of heavy things. An activity which the Princess would never consider.

Shmate: Derived from the Yiddish word for rag. The kind of old clothes a Princess simply wouldn't wear.

Svelte: Antonym for zaftig. Flat chested, full hipped Princess who survives on M&Ms and TAB.

T t

TAB: The all-occasion beverage. Poured with meat, fish and Sarah Lee cheesecake.

Taste: That which keeps the Princess from being not merely spoiled but highly selective. Cannot be learned. Instinctive.

Tepel: The proverbial pot in which to make chicken soup.

Tsachkes: Knick-knacks made of glass, crystal, marble and china that cover every square inch of available space in the Palace.

Wedding: The Main Event. Ceremony for which the Princess has been primed since birth. Also refers to lavish affair which could send her father to the poorhouse.

Wholesale: Favored method for the Princess to obtain all goods.

Work: Word not in the Princess' vocabulary, especially when it includes the prefix "house."

Yuppulas: Derived from the word Yuppies. Young urban Jewish professionals. Refers to both Princes and Princesses.

ZEEB: (ZBT) Members of the Zeta Beta Tau fraternity. 16.3% grow up to be attorneys, 12.9% grow up to be physicians or dentists, 17.4% grow up to be CPAs, 22.2% grow up to be stock brokers and 31.2% never grow up.

Zaftig: Epithet used to describe Princesses with a pretty face and a figure that boasts a buxum bosom, generous belly and spindly legs. The product of generations of Eastern European genes.

The Closet Balabusta

There is in the mind of every Princess, a corner in which the following phrases lurk. But a modern day Princess would chalish* if any of them slipped out in everyday speech.

Balabusta: The perfect Jewish homemaker who cooks and cleans from dawn to dusk and has her elderly mother-in-law living in the guest bedroom. "She's a real balabusta," although she may seem sweet and meek from all outward appearances, don't cross this Princess because she might tell you to . . .

Chubs dier in bud: Similar to the English phrase, "Go soak your head." Literally, "Go sit in the tub." (Variation: In shteb afen abershten bonk . . . "You should sit in the steam on the top bench where the steam is the hottest.")

Ein se zachen: Both of you go hang yourself with a rope, one at each end.

Ver ge shvollen: You should swell up.

Ver fabrentz: You should burn up.

Shlugs ze kup in de vant: Go hit your head on the wall.

Hoch mir in chenick: Stop hitting the teacup.

Zol nor shtinken from dine kup und dine fees: You should stink from your head and your feet.

Vox vie a tzibel mit 'en kup in derard: You should grow like an onion with your head in the ground.